'An inspiring story of searching for joy and ilst weathering the storms of life. Thr... in, Emma's faith provides us wit... ur fears and deliver healing for ...
                    Heidi ...*icer, MAMA Academy*

'Emma writes with a raw authenticity to show how a test became a testimony of God's grace. Through a journey of heartache and challenges, Emma discovered hope in the midst of the pain and sadness. This is an incredible story and as you read it you will be encouraged, find strength and know that you too can discover hope for today and the days ahead.'

Helen Roberts, Executive Minister,
Wellspring Church, and author

'One after another, the trials just seem to keep coming with every one of Emma's children. This is a story of perseverance and of the power of God's promises to sustain through the heartbreak.'

Tania Harris, pastor, speaker, author, and director,
GodConversations.com

'Emma has such a beautiful and authentic story of the testimony of God's goodness in the midst of obstacles. She believed God through the storms. This story brings faith to those who may have lost hope and the faith to believe God can do anything!'

Jurgen Matthesius, Senior Pastor, C3 San Diego

'With colourful and descriptive illustrations drawn from her life journey, Emma's book evokes deep compassion and empathy, while highlighting the incredible supernatural hope and courage found in the presence and promises of God. Such a beautiful and impacting book.'

Helen Monk, Equippers Church pastor

'Unconditional love means, "affection without limitations". Emma questions this through her own anxieties. Her hope gives her the strength to fight for her family. Controlling and fixing children is something I've seen in families' through work. I respect how Emma found a way to guide hers through difficult times. A book that will empower you to see the "importance of positive thinking".'

Sian Jones, West Surrey Manager, Surrey Care Trust

Stretched

Baby loss, autism, illness – a mother's true story of hope and survival

Emma Rutland

Authentic

First published 2019 by Authentic Media Limited,
PO Box 6326, Bletchley, Milton Keynes, MK1 9GG.
authenticmedia.co.uk

British Library Cataloguing in Publication Data
A catalogue record for this book is available from the British Library.
ISBN: 978-1-78893-039-0
978-1-78893-040-6 (e-book)

Cover design by Vivian Hansen
Printed and bound by CPI Group (UK) Ltd., Croydon, CR0 4YY

I dedicate this book to my lovely family.

Andy, you've lived this story too, thank you for providing for us and committing your life to us. I love you. Zoe, Daniel, Georgia and Jasmine, you have been a gift to me. Thank you for enriching my life. I am privileged and very grateful to be your mum.

Contents

Foreword

I've known the Rutland family for a number years. I know their story. I've been an onlooker and, on a few rare occasions, a participator in some of the challenges Emma writes about. Despite that knowledge, I was not prepared for the visceral impact this book would make on me. It starts off 'homey', like an episode of *Little House on the Prairie*. I felt safe, secure, in known territory. But then the horror strikes. It is raw, emotional and at times brutal, yet honest throughout. Emma does not present herself as a modern saint. She has more in common with the hero of *The Pilgrim's Progress* who fought, struggled and many times wanted to give up on life. Nevertheless he kept moving towards the Celestial City.

This account will take you on a journey marked by pain, loss and tragedy few of us could handle. And every time you read of another monster rising up from the deep to swallow this woman, this family, you will marvel at the courage of Emma to continue, despite her brokenness and pain. She shows a level of vulnerability and openness in her writing I rarely see. I'm touched. I'm inspired. I want to do better myself having read her story. The title says it all! But this is also a story of hope, of healing, of deep connection and appreciation – for family, life and a God who is good.

The story of Jesus is similar. He said yes to embracing limitations in his life in order to bring life, forgiveness and healing to others. John puts it like this: 'the Word became flesh and dwelt among us . . . we have beheld his glory . . . ' (John 1:14, RSV). This 'yes' to limitation opened Jesus up to many possibilities. Beauty, friendship, loyalty, love and appreciation were part of his world. But it also opened him to the possibility of pain, loss, tragedy, betrayal and even death. He is called by one prophet 'a man of sorrows . . . acquainted with grief' (Isa. 53:3, RSV). Jesus gets it. He's experienced it. Still, his death wasn't the end of the story. The resurrection is proof that God can bring life out of any tragedy or loss.

Emma's story is a testament to this truth. Her joy is genuine. Her healing is real. Her family are terrific. For those of you struggling with similar circumstances in life, take heart from reading this book. You'll cry. I did. But you'll also feel hope rise, and that gives birth to joy. For those of you who don't face the same issues as Emma but have your own dragons to slay, be inspired by her courage to not give up. There is a way forward. For those of you who feel trapped with no way of escape, take Emma's advice and get help. It's out there. And for those of you who live incredibly blessed lives with none of these heartaches, thank God.

Peter Prothero MA
Senior Pastor
Equippers Church London

Preface

Rainbows are so beautiful. I love how the colours wash into each other, each creating its own hue from one shade to the next. As the sun shines and the rain pelts down, the intensity of colour attracts me and touches something deep within me; maybe it's because of their vibrancy, or maybe it's their beauty amidst a storm that makes me notice them. I am captivated, feeling hope and joy when I see them – but there is more to it than vibrancy and beauty; there is a much deeper cause for my joy. Promises. Faithful, tangible and true promises that have been illustrated by rainbows. Promises that have drawn me towards hope and directed me away from fear. I have had moments in my life when I just needed a sign to get me through a difficult time, and miraculously, in those times, I have been gifted with the splendour of a rainbow, which has brought colour and hope into my stormy world. Rainbows have been a treasure to me.

The purpose of writing this book is to implant hope into brokenness through sharing my story. I have found beauty out of sadness and hope springing out of the fragmentation as the sun illuminates the rain.

I am a wife, to Andy, and mother of four children: Zoe, Daniel, Georgia and Jasmine. I hope that as you read this book you are inspired to believe you are capable of achieving anything, capable of overcoming everything; that you have been made with purpose, destiny and everlasting hope, despite any storm that might try to convince you otherwise.

I would like to share a little snapshot of my story with you – the joy and the pain, the lessons and beliefs that have shaped my journey. Life is so colourful and as we experience it, we can all tell important and unique stories of how we have been shaped to be the people we are today. My story tells of loss, caring for a child with medical problems and bringing up a child with special needs, but also of how I have searched for gold and found the sun shining through the rain.

Gold is precious and valuable. As I have met people and heard their stories, I have come to learn that this is true of us too. We are all precious and valuable, and I believe that we all have treasure within us. Our 'gold' is our ability to love and value others and ourselves. For some of us, though, our gold has become hidden by difficult life experiences and it no longer shines out. It is unseen and, when no one notices it, we find ourselves feeling worthless and unloved. A little kindness, gentleness and belief from others can help us rediscover it.

Sadly, in our society we are surrounded by a belief system that tells us we aren't quite good enough, we have failed, and we feel worthless if we don't measure up to the culture we have created.

I believe this is an illusion. Who has authority over our culture, and why do many of us struggle with self-worth and failed expectations? I believe that everyone has purpose and value, and I think it is important to challenge a culture that has us doubting ourselves and that says we're never quite enough.

More than sixteen years ago, I found myself in a place that I had not chosen or expected to be in, and it floored me. It wasn't the first time I had been knocked down and it certainly wasn't going to be the last, but it was from this position that an idea was planted in my mind that I would one day write my story. I began to write journals to record what was happening, and this quickly became a form of therapy rather than a discipline. Some days I would write reams trying to figure out what was going on in my life; other days would pass by unwritten and unaccounted for. My moments were being recorded for a future purpose, and I had no idea what would transpire during that time, or even how long it would all last; but the idea took root and has grown and has brought me to today.

The journey I am going to share with you has been fraught with challenges, and sometimes life has seemed very dark; but my message is one of hope and of restoration as I have learnt to engage with pain in the present, alongside daring to embrace the future of my purpose and destiny.

Emma
www.emmarutland.co.uk

The Rutland Family, 2017

1

Words

'You're ugly, do you know that?' His eyes glinted, and he spoke in hushed tones so he wouldn't be heard by the teacher, who was taking the afternoon register. There was something very cold in his expression and I froze. I did not know how to respond. I felt like I had been stabbed.

I was 10 years old.

Four years later I was in the science lab, and there was a general ripple of noise as everyone exchanged ideas about the task the teacher had given. The room was filled with the dim smell of Bunsen gas from past experiments. Each workbench was littered with printed worksheets, graffiti-decorated pencil cases and the occasional green gas tap. We were adorned with the school laboratory coats which no longer had their fresh, white, starched, professional look. Mine had grubby sleeves and a frilly hole at the side seam, which looked like a bullet had passed through it. It was a little on the tight side for me, being fuller in the chest than most. It irritated me how the buttons stressed in their holes and the gaps between them wanted to arch out, making more of my size than I wanted to show. It seemed to me that everyone else looked great in theirs and they could apply themselves to learning and interacting with one another, undistracted by their appearance.

A bustle of movement lifted me from my thoughts, and as everyone got up from their seats I wondered what instruction I'd missed while I was doing this self-assessment. An all-too-familiar sinking feeling pricked my emotions as I saw people beginning to form into groups; that feeling of being excluded because I didn't quite fit in. The silent words in my mind – 'loner', 'weirdo' – made me wish I was someone else, anyone else but me. I wanted to be one of the popular girls. I wanted to at least feel that I fitted somewhere.

As the hubbub settled down, the teacher ushered me into a group full of faces that seemed less than pleased about me joining them. Maybe my presence unsettled their equilibrium or status somehow. I had no idea. Nonetheless, here I was, so I thought I'd better knuckle down and engage in the moment. We were presented with a series of glass dishes, bottles of clear liquid and some lumps of metal, with the expectation that we could somehow make a series of conclusions about how they reacted when put together. I was assigned to distribute the dishes. As I was handing them out, one of the boys in my group walked up behind me, leaned in to take his dish, pressed himself against me and in a hot breath whispered in my ear, 'You're dead ugly, you are.' Shocked to be hearing these words spoken so directly to me, my mind flickered to that memory four years ago.

I couldn't believe that I was hearing these words for a second time. My heart sank and my throat constricted. I felt ashamed, insignificant and worthless. Who really cared about metal reactions in the face of such rejection? I wanted to get out of there. I hated this place. It was rubbish. School was meant to be a place of revelation and learning. It should have been exciting and fun but, for me, it represented all the things that I felt I could never be and things I thought I could never have. I wanted to be accepted and to belong. I wanted to be valued, not feel isolated and abnormal. Surely in this room packed with people, full of opinions and differences, there was someone with a little compassion, someone who could see value in me and who wanted to be my friend?

Ugly. A simple word that holds so much – rejection, pain, loneliness, worthlessness. What was this boy actually saying to me? Was he trying to say he didn't want me to be in his group, or was he really making a statement about my appearance? At the age of 14, what I heard was that my face was not acceptable, that I was not acceptable.

I did not respond outwardly to his remark; I let no expression show. No one could see the pain from the dagger that had just pierced my heart. I gave nothing away and continued with the task. The moment passed, unnoticed by everyone else in the room, but this left me with a deep wound that was to define my future choices.

There are moments in our lives that somehow point us in certain directions, this was one of those for me. I was crushed and here a belief took root that I was ugly and undesirable to others. I was a reject.

One of the ways I coped with rejection was to dream I was somewhere else. I knew what I desired above anything else in life, so I created a fantasy world that I could live in.

There was a stillness in my bedroom which was peaceful and calm. To the left of the bed was a little cot with a doll and, next to that, a chest of drawers on top of which was a pile of little clothes and a hamster cage. I would change the doll's clothes and place her in the cot. I would put a bottle to her mouth when I had finished my homework. As I did my homework, the silence was occasionally broken by the tapping sound of the hamster licking his water bottle. I would stop what I was doing to take him out of his cage. His whiskers would twitch as I lifted him out to kiss him and give him some love.

My maternal instinct was strong and I played with baby dolls into my early teens. I always took an interest in babies and sometimes helped out in a crèche. I felt content when I could nurture and love, both in the fantasy of playing with dolls and in the reality of looking after my hamster. Part of me wished it was different, but for most of my teenage years I chose a life of isolation from others, keeping to myself and rarely socializing. I felt safer that way.

On a number of levels, rejection broke into my world of naivety and it hurt so much. But it also planted within me a strong determination not be taken down by it. Little did I know that my imagination, my place of contentment and my heart's desire would have a huge significance in shaping my future.

When it came time for me to leave home, the wardrobe doors were open, revealing an empty shell of wood inside. The clothes rail was slightly bowed and, at its deepest point, a collection of bare hangers huddled together. This chapter of my life was about to close. On the unmade bed lay a large brown suitcase, with zips bulging, the expansion zip fully open. It was holding the contents of my life. An adventure was just beginning and the time had come to say 'goodbye' to the old and 'hello' to the new.

My excitement was bubbling and yet I felt nervous. I had high expectations and I had pinned my hopes on this next move. The papers had come through, it was official, I had passed my exams and I was on my way to nursing college, which was 200 miles away. I was 18 years old and I was done with fantasy; I needed life to be fuller. I wanted to find a place where I felt that I belonged. I wanted to have friends and be a part of something that made me feel whole, and I wanted to meet a man who I could settle down with and ultimately, have a family with. I had no idea what lay ahead, but the plan was now in action!

The car was full. It was going to transport me and all the things I would need to set up a simple life away from home. My only brother, Mat, and I were squeezed in the back between boxes and bedding and my mum and dad filled the front spaces. It was going to be a while until we were all together again. I fixed my gaze on my home as we pulled away; it held many memories, some good and some bad, but I felt content to be leaving it behind.

We arrived before nightfall on a blustery Sunday in September. The buildings around me seemed tired and run-down. The car park was full of free spaces and there didn't seem to be much going on. We pulled into a parking space beside a small building, which appeared to be the check-in destination, according to my letter of acceptance.

We climbed out of the car and stretched after our long journey. The reality of the situation dawned on me and my mouth felt dry. The room we entered was dull and unimpressive and felt impersonal. My decision to start this nursing course was very much in question at this point, but I pushed myself forward to make my introductions. There was a girl called Steph signing in at the same time as me. I think we must have sent silent signals across the room, assuring each other, 'We are in this together.' Steph and I would become firm friends for many years. We had passed the first level of initiation of signing papers and next we were handed the keys to our accommodation. This was the place where I was to live for the next three years. My new life was about to begin and I somehow knew that it would never be the same again.

2

Andy

Fuelled by alcohol, I reached up and kissed him! He seemed stunned; in fact, I took myself by surprise as I had never kissed someone like that before! He kissed me back, so all was well.

We were at a popular nightclub which had recently been renovated. It was dark, and we had queued for a short while before we could go in, and as usual I had been challenged for identification as I looked young for my age. As we entered, a large spacious room opened up in front of me; there were no windows and spotlights of various colours lit the room. Clouds of cigarette smoke swirled under the spotlights and stung my eyes as I blinked to adjust to the darkness. There was an area in the middle of the room for dancing, and it was full of lively people grooving to the beat of the music. My friend Jenny and I left the boys to get drinks while we took to the dance floor. I felt intimidated as I was not very well coordinated, so I watched the people around me to see how they danced and to see if I could mimic what they were doing. Jenny used her arms a lot when she danced, but I found it tricky to move my legs and my arms at the same time. Some people jumped, and some just stepped to the left and to the right and back again, with their arms beside them – I could copy that! I was grateful for the drink the boys brought back with them, as it helped me to relax and feel less stupid. I began to enjoy the scene, and after a while I felt so alive. I started to lose the inhibitions I once had. We danced lots and drank lots, and I really got into the swing of things. I actually forgot I had come in with the boys, and when I realized I was missing them I went to find them. I could only find Andy, and that was when I had kissed him. By the end of the evening it seemed we had made a connection neither of us had expected to make, and it had all started twenty-four hours earlier.

It had been a chilly Friday evening in early January. We had pulled into the pub car park, and as I climbed out of the back seat and my eyes scanned the view, I sensed that Alan, Jenny and I wouldn't be alone in the crowd that evening. Sure enough, my eyes fell upon the figure of a young, tall, brown-haired man. He was sauntering over to us. He wore jeans and a top, which suited his slim build. His eyes were blue like mine, and his clean-shaven face had gentle features. He seemed to know Alan, and it quickly became clear to me that a double date had been planned without my knowledge! I shyly greeted him as he smiled at me, and the four of us ambled over to the entrance of the pub. The room was brimming with people, and smoke filled the place, giving faces a hazy outline as I looked around for the bar. We politely pushed our way through the masses and waited our turn to order the drinks. The noise level of music and chatter was high, and I strained my ears to hear our conversations, smiling sweetly at times, in pretence of knowing what had just been uttered and hoping that the smile was an appropriate facial gesture! The evening passed by uneventfully, but we had all enjoyed ourselves and left feeling happy and connected. Jenny teased me with her assurance that Andy 'liked' me and that I should watch this space, but I hadn't been so sure. When I kissed him the next evening, it put a whole new light on the situation!

On Sunday, I spent the day sleeping off my hangover and contemplated what had happened over the weekend. By the evening, I was dressed, had something to eat and was beginning to prepare for the week ahead when I heard a knock on my door. I opened it and there stood Andy. He looked sheepish and tired as he awkwardly asked to come in. I wasn't feeling quite as bold as the night before, and I felt a little embarrassed about my forward behaviour, so I hesitantly invited him in.

My simple room in 'I block' was rectangular in shape; it was furnished with a bed, a dresser, a table, a chair and a cupboard, and there was a little sink in the corner. The walls were painted magnolia and the window had two floral floor-to-ceiling curtains hanging over it. I had tried to jolly the room up with a bright red duvet cover and I had put a couple of pictures up on the plain walls. I think these gave it a more homely feel. I showed Andy to the hard chair in the corner and wondered what was going to happen next.

We chatted briefly about the night before and then he asked me a question I had not been anticipating.

'Will you go out with me?' I wasn't sure about the forty-eight hours that had preceded this and I'm not particularly proud of what I said next.

'No.'

The response just hung there for a moment as he absorbed the answer. The conversation and chatter we had just shared drew to an abrupt halt, and before I knew it, I was standing alone in my room again, in a kind of stunned state. I felt like I had been cruel to him, but maybe it was better to end it before it got started, so I comforted myself that little damage had been done, as so little had been invested.

I spent the next few days questioning myself about whether it was the right thing to have done. I couldn't get it out of my head. I had spent years wondering if anyone would like me after the 'ugly' comments and, aside from the few boys I had had a short on/off thing with, this was the first time 'the chase' had happened in any measurable way. This was what I'd moved 200 miles away from home for, wasn't it? OK, so nurse training was *how* I happened to be here, but *why* I was here was a completely different thing. I was on the hunt for a man; I was looking for someone I could marry and have babies with! Had I just closed the door on my future? Maybe I shouldn't have been so hasty!

Was it too late to change my mind? Poor Andy being sent away like that – would he be interested in me now, after being rejected? He seemed a decent and lovely person from what I knew, so I came to the conclusion that I should apologize and sent word via Jenny to Alan to Andy that I had changed my mind and that we should at least give it a go!

Fortunately, Andy agreed to meet me again. I mused with Jenny on what kind of low-key date we could have. She suggested somewhere like the cinema where conversation didn't need to take high precedence, somewhere we could just be relaxed and take it slowly. Perhaps another double date too, that would take off the pressure and at least I'd know about it this time!

After a few more evenings out with Andy, Jenny and Alan, I felt I didn't need the safety of double dates any more, so we began to spend time alone together, and my relationship with Andy grew stronger. As the months passed by, I found I enjoyed spending time with him, and when we were apart, I counted the hours till we would be together again.

One evening the following spring, we had been invited to celebrate his mum's birthday at a lovely Italian restaurant.

The menu invited me to order everything, but I had to make a choice and, unbeknown to me, that wasn't the only choice I was going to make that evening.

The meal did not disappoint, and it would have been rude to pass on desserts, so we ordered them too. As they came, instead of starting his, Andy got off his chair and knelt down on the floor beside me. At first, I wondered if he had he dropped something, but it didn't take me too long to notice that he was opening a small black box with a beautiful, diamond-cluster engagement ring inside and was asking me to marry him!

By this point, Andy was my close companion. He was an answer to my prayers for a lifelong partner who loved me and wanted to have a family with me. I adored him. This time I was sure of my response.

'Yes!'

3

Nurse Training and Marriage

We sat in the staffroom, and my eyes were glazed from the early start. In my hands, I held a pen and a scrap piece of paper, to take notes of the names and conditions of the people currently sleeping on the ward.

'Vera, 78 years old. Admitted yesterday with breathing problems, history of lung disease. Observe and medicate for pneumonia and nebulisers. Awaiting X-ray results.'

'Elsie, 52 years. Admitted two weeks ago, myocardial infarction (heart attack). Doing well. Home later if physio report OK. Send drug chart for medication to take home.'

'Cynthia, 83 years . . . diabetic . . .'

It was still dark outside, and my tummy grumbled with the knowledge that it would be hours before I could eat something. I was assigned to the six-bedded ladies' bay with Staff Nurse Sarah. She was experienced, on the ball and knew how to direct the students in order to get the most out of their placements. I soon forgot my hunger, and started to help the ladies get up and washed for the day; then I took their general health observations and followed Sarah with the drug trolley. The doctors swept in and out during this time, and I caught some of the conversations and plans for the ladies to aid their recovery so they could get their tickets out of there.

The day ticked on – my breakfast break turned into a brunch break, and on my return to the ladies' bay, Elsie was back in bed, and I noticed her face was not a good colour. Her eyes were closed and her hands were interlocked, resting over her chest. I approached her with concern, saying her name a couple of times before I reached out and touched her. She did not respond. Panic arose within me; I knew this was not OK, but I had no clue what to do next. I called out to Sarah, who must have read from my voice something wasn't right as she raced over and pulled the emergency button above the bed. We unlocked the wheels of the bed, dragged it out and pulled off the headboard. Sarah had assessed very quickly that Elsie's heart had stopped and I was about to learn the motions of resuscitation. There was no time to check my textbook! My tutor was Sarah and several doctors had also joined us. After watching the others before me, I was shown how to hold my hands together in the form of a fist over Elsie's chest and to push with all my might in rhythmic form. It wasn't long before I was tiring and the motion had to be taken over by another person. Our team worked together with a good result as Elsie's heart responded to the treatment. Her heart began to beat on its own again, and we stepped back to see how she was faring with her other bodily functions. The observations showed that she was unable to breathe on her own, so she was transferred to intensive care for ventilation therapy.

This whirlwind and hasty exit had left the room in stunned silence. The gravity of what had just happened had affected everyone. Elsie's dance with death had a deep impact on me and sobered my fairy-tale notion of being a lovely, caring nurse whose smile was part of the treatment in making people better. I knew now that this was a great responsibility and something to be taken very seriously. I matured a great deal that day; in that moment my naivety was challenged and I realized how little I knew and how unprepared I was.

I faced many challenges as I trained, some I didn't enjoy so much and some I embraced. One of the things I really enjoyed during nurse training was teaching people to manage their new pattern of life after they had life-changing surgery or a life-changing medical event. I learnt how important it was to know as much as you could and to be able to accept and deal with change so you could be as independent as possible. I suppose this side of the job fitted with my instinct to nurture. Part of my job was to devise a teaching package for people who had recently been diagnosed with diabetes. I was to design some material which could be used to show someone how to test their blood sugar levels so they could calculate how much insulin they would need to inject. I was praised for my efforts and I was delighted. I didn't know how significant this skill would be to me later in my life.

Three years of training passed. It had been full of challenges and I had learnt a lot, not only in the area of medical knowledge but also in the area of personal development. I had learnt much about the dynamics of relationships. I had made good decisions and also some bad decisions, which I was able to work through with the support of my colleagues and friends. I had gained wisdom about life which was to equip me for my future.

I was now a qualified nurse, I had met Andy, got engaged and bought my first home. My life was barely recognizable from the place I had begun. The anxious trainee nurse in the empty car park by the rundown hospital buildings seemed far away. I had made some deep-rooted friendships and I reflected with my friend Steph how far we had come as a group and as individuals. Life was about to take another turn, and I was ready to embrace my future with Andy, as we made our vows to one another.

On my wedding day, the beeping of the alarm clock woke me with a start. It felt like I'd only just fallen asleep as I rubbed the dust from my eyes. I began to realize what this day had in store for me. I became mindful of a growing nervous excitement as it dawned on me that today I was getting married.

The daylight was shining through a crack in the curtains that hung in Mum and Dad's spare room. It cast a bright line across the desk. I grimaced and shifted my squinting eyes to my beautiful bridal gown hanging on the back of the door. I lay there and shut my eyes again for a while, reflecting on how I'd got to this point and I dreamed of the life that lay ahead. I wondered if I would be happy, if I would have the children I'd hoped for and what life would be like once I was a married woman. I had grown to love Andy deeply, he had become my close friend and I cherished him in my heart. I believed we were meant to be together, and this day was a celebration of my commitment to him. I was 21 years old – I was so young, yet I felt so very grown up. Today was my fairy-tale day, the day I had dreamed of for much of my childhood. I was going to be a princess in my lacy bridal gown and marry my prince in his top hat and tails!

In the room next to mine and from the kitchen below me, I began to hear movement – the household rousing, and I guessed Fiona, my bridesmaid, and my mum and dad were awake. The day had begun! I threw back my covers, swung my legs out of bed and placed my feet on the floor. My body flew upright with the momentum. The door started to open slowly and on seeing that I was awake, a very excited Fiona entered saying, 'Happy wedding day!' We embraced each other, jumped up and down and broke into songs about weddings and bells chiming! Our laughter and excitement mingled with the smell of toast; we needed to fill our energy stores for the day ahead.

We headed downstairs together, bubbling with conversation about flowers, hairdressers, timings, wedding cars and guests. Mum and Dad beamed at us. The room was filled with pride and gladness and I felt supported in my decision to marry Andy.

As breakfast finished, we scattered to gather everything we needed for the day – we were to travel nearer to the church, to the house of a friend, for the final preparations. When we arrived, the house was warm, spacious and welcoming and the occupants had vacated it to give us some space to get ready. My other two bridesmaids also joined me, along with the flowers, the hairdresser and the photographer. The mood was light and it was a joyous time.

By the afternoon, I was wearing my long, ivory gown with a fitted bodice that bounced out just below my waist. Layers of lace were strategically sewn around my neckline which took the attention away from my large chest, which I was very self-conscious about. The lower skirt of the dress flared out with lots of volume and reached the floor. My make-up was simple. My face was lightly touched with foundation, I wore peachy eyeshadow to enhance my blue eyes and rouged my cheeks for a more defined look. My painted lips glimmered as I looked into the mirror and pouted. The hairdresser had scooped my long hair into an upwards gathering with curls cascading down my back. A simple floral band anchored my veil which fell lightly across my face. I felt and looked beautiful.

This moment was heavy with significance. It proved to me that the lies I'd believed about not being good enough or pretty enough to the outside world, simply weren't true. I had been chosen and today I would celebrate for a number of different reasons.

My dad beamed with pride as I stepped out of the house to walk towards the waiting car. Nerves jittered as I realized the attention of our wedding guests would be focused on me, a position I wasn't entirely comfortable with, but I knew it was all part of the occasion to announce our love to the people we had invited to celebrate with us.

The first bars of the Trumpet Voluntary resounded as I began my advance down the aisle. I could see Andy's face fixed to my moving frame and I could see him mouth the word, 'Beautiful.' A joy rose within me. The church was full of happy faces and warmth towards us. I was blessed to be marrying someone who loved me so much. I was thankful to have so many friends and family in one place. I was delighted to receive good wishes for a long and happy marriage. I believed that this moment had been ordained by a God who really cared about me as an individual. My faith was something that had brought me to this day. My life had been shaped around a Christian faith from the day I was born. Both sets of grandparents and my parents had chosen to follow the guidelines from the Bible. They had decided to use Jesus' example of serving others and loving them no matter who they were or what they had done. This way of life seemed to make sense to me and I had chosen to adopt this as my own too. Andy's family had attended church for as long as he could remember also.

Ahead of us, mounted on the wall at the front of the church was a wall-hanging my mum had made which said, 'Andy and Emma, joined in His love' with two interlinking hearts. There was a real sense of intimacy and it felt so personal to us. My uncle, an ordained Baptist minister, took the service and some friends played the music. It really was the fairy tale I had dreamt of!

I was 21, with my whole life in front of me, and I was convinced that marrying Andy was the right thing to do. I had no idea what lay ahead for us both, but I knew the decision I had made was full of hope and destiny, and if hope and destiny weren't enough, then weathering the storms of life would soon put this to the test!

There was bliss in our young marriage. Hopes and expectations were high. This was a new beginning, full of opportunities. We were in love and fully invested in our journey together. Andy was studying for his accountancy exams, and I was a newly qualified nurse. Our home was a place filled with love. It was a safe haven to nurture each other in our desires and dreams for the future.

But this was not to last for long.

4

Miscarriage and God

Wouldn't it be great to suspend time when life is going well? To take a snapshot and acknowledge the huge blessing of the moment? These moments are a treasure. They are an investment to draw upon when the time changes. The storm will come, whoever or wherever you are, as this is the nature of life on this earth. Not that we should expect with gloom that life will go 'pear shaped', but we can expect challenges to come our way and when they do, we need to know that we have the resources to face them.

For my husband and I, something began to change – tension began to creep into our safe, fairy-tale haven. I found nursing hugely stressful. The long hours, the shift work, the politics and the aching feet! We were constantly understaffed and my inexperience led me to the belief that I wasn't good enough, which put a huge strain on me. Responsibility for people's lives lay in my hands and sometimes, it was *only* my hands. It was a heavy burden to carry. The possibility of a fatal mistake lay just in front of me and a lack of self-belief began to grow.

I started to carry the heaviness of fear around. It came with me wherever I went – I could feel it at home, at work and in my friendships and I could not shift it. Fear fuelled my belief that I wasn't good enough and that I was going to make a massive error if I carried on nursing. Fear was in control and, in the end, it robbed me of my nursing career. A year and a quarter after I had qualified, I gave up my job because I was so unhappy. I had become disillusioned about what I hoped would be a caring profession. Perhaps I would have made an excellent nurse if things had been different and if I'd had more support, confidence and self-belief. I was at an all-time low.

Six months previously, Andy and I had thought we would be embarking on a new journey after receiving a positive pregnancy test. But when we had the twelve-week scan, this dream was shattered as I was told I had a blighted ovum – which is when a pregnancy sac develops but the baby does not. I was devastated. The gloom and despair was overwhelming. Not only was I not going to be a mum this time, but I also didn't have a reason to get out of nursing. I didn't feel I should just give up work and do nothing at home, but I found I could not carry on. So, with Andy's blessing, I quit my job. I was broken. I wanted to stop the world and get off.

Upset and angry, I cried out to the God I'd always believed to be loving, kind and full of hope. 'How could you? You're so cruel! If this is what you do to people, I don't want to know you or be associated with you! You're out of my life.'

Now that I had given up work and was at home, I had plenty of time to think. I remember thinking of scenarios which fitted in with my image of God. I had always pictured him in a positive way. I had been taught that he was loving, gentle, kind, slow to anger and victorious in battle. The idea of him being cruel and wicked towards me didn't fit with my original picture. I wondered what else I was supposed to think of him. My spinning thoughts led me to decide that God just didn't exist. If there was no God, then there would be nobody to blame for bad things and no point in having hope set on something that wasn't really there. I decided that must be it. There was nothing beyond me.

I needed time to heal and I knew that I needed to get pregnant again. I became self-absorbed; I had to find inner strength because I was on my own. I was determined that I would not let myself down. I tried to make myself believe the world and everything around me was just the result of some random event. I tried to believe that this is our one life, that it serves no eternal purpose, and we must just try to make the best of it. The process of time took my thoughts further down the road until I was struck by the thought that if God didn't exist, what about people who were traumatized by life? What about those who were abused or those who had lost children or parents? That was hell on earth. What about people who lived in torment until death took them – all this and for what purpose? It didn't make sense to me. I battled back and forth in my mind for weeks. One day I would believe there was a God who was good, as I had originally believed; the next day I would question if there was a God at all. Then I would think, 'If God does exist, he must not care about us, or perhaps he sends bad things our way.'

As the days went on and I tossed these questions about, I found that I began to think more of a God who was good, rather than being non-existent or cruel. I also began to think there may be another force working against this good God that was the root of bad things. This seemed to make more sense to me than any of my other reasonings. I eventually came to the conclusion that God did exist, and I chose to stick with that. I believed there was something that was bigger than me and maybe my struggle was because I had misunderstood him. My faith was growing. I yearned to explore more. I needed to find out more about God and this other force, whatever that may be.

At the same time, I was becoming increasingly frustrated and confused by not getting what I felt was owed to me. Women conceived and had babies all the time, didn't they? Why hadn't this happened for me? I was in a committed relationship, I had a strong maternal drive and a lovely home in which to bring up a child. How did God fit in with all of this? What did I need, and why was I searching?

In time, I stopped blaming God for the loss of my baby and I began to ask some different questions, questions that were a lot bigger than just me and my world. I made a choice to engage in something that was to provide me with more information about God and also a place for open discussions. I enrolled on the Alpha course. This course was being run by volunteers at the church I attended. I felt safe and accepted for who I was. I felt free to ask questions about what I was really thinking, and share my disappointments. I was able to find out more about who God really is.

The forum here was the right shape for me. I began to grapple with a new concept of God. The picture I had of God expanded, and I began to see a God who fights with this other 'force' and breaks into suffering bringing transformation and new life. He had allowed nature to take its course when I had lost my baby. But then he showed me something bigger and better about who he was and how he cares for us and gives strength and power into our lives. I discovered how God works within our suffering, in the midst of lost dreams and when we are experiencing heartache. I got to know a God who knew all about suffering, but he was victorious over death. I also began to see that there was a bigger picture – a picture other than the one I was experiencing. Even though it was awful and I felt so sad, I knew I wouldn't always be in this place.

I started to see God as a nurturer. I could see his heart was broken by my pain, and how he longed for me to experience healing. In my case, it was emotional healing. I began to believe that God could rebuild lives that had crumbled beneath the weight of the troubles that had been heaped upon them. He could turn it all around and somehow build new, bigger and better lives, if only we allowed him to do so.

It was during this search for God that I was blessed to become pregnant again. I had been instilled with a new sense of hope, but without the element of assumption – I now knew that these things were not a 'given'. This time, I knew it could go wrong. I was also conscious that I had learnt something – life didn't owe me anything, and having a child would be a gift.

It was also around this time that I began to develop a deep friendship. Julie was ahead of me in life's journey as far as family goes. Her daughter Amy was 1 year old, with beautiful blonde, curly hair. I was honoured to spend time with them during the long months of pregnancy while I waited for my turn to receive my bundle of joy. Julie was carrying her own bundle of joy and was due within days from me.

Throughout my pregnancy, I was aware of the vulnerability of life. I would like to say that I was OK with this, but as the pregnancy progressed, the underlying fear of loss was growing too. I had heard of stillbirth; it had happened to a family in the church several years back.

'Please God, don't let that happen to me.'

While there were moments of fear during my pregnancy, I wasn't overwhelmed with it. The moments were fleeting, and perhaps it was good for me to learn to trust that God would provide. It was perfectly normal to worry. Besides which, when Andy and I had been on holiday in France, we were in a little village and we saw some building blocks with the name 'Zoe' on them in a shop window. That was the name we had chosen if we were to have a girl. The name 'Zoe' means 'life'.

Peace was with me.

5

Motherhood

November 1996 saw my desire to be a mother fulfilled when Zoe Clare was born. She weighed a healthy 8lb 1oz. We were overjoyed – we had a baby girl to nurture, teach and love. I truly felt that I had begun to live out the purpose for which I'd been born.

An idyllic year followed. We had the usual sleepless nights, the odd illness and overnight trip to hospital, but for the most part, it was a joyful and satisfying year. We watched with anticipation and pride as Zoe grew and achieved her milestones. Each event brought us our own little gift of joy as her doting parents.

Maternal emotions are a strange thing. As Zoe turned 1, my mind was consumed with a yearning to have more children. When I had been younger, I had dreamt of having four children, and this seemed to take over any sensible rationale about what the reality of this might look like.

I was fortunate to become pregnant again quite quickly, and I looked forward with less trepidation this time. I was armed with the 'I've done it before and it all worked' attitude, and the fear of loss I had known during my pregnancy with Zoe was very much at bay. However, occasionally, I did like to check everything was OK with the stethoscope I owned from my days in nursing. At our 21-week scan, we discovered all was well and that we were going to have a baby boy. I was grateful that our baby was well but, to be honest, I wasn't very sure about him being a boy! My relationship with my father and brother hadn't been good, and my experience of the 'male kind' told me to be wary. Emotionally, I had some work to do. We felt a name was a good place to start, so we decided our son was to be called Daniel. As the pregnancy progressed, I reflected on experiences with men I had had in the past.

I didn't see much of my dad when I was a child as he worked long hours and our chances to build relationship were challenged by a lack of time. When Dad was around, we did attempt to create some sort of connection. On a few occasions, he would swing me and my brother in a holdall bag over the banister as he sang, 'What shall we do with the drunken sailor?' I thought it was great fun, until one day he said he couldn't swing me in the bag any more because I was too heavy. Of course, this seems reasonable now, but at the time, I just didn't understand. I thought he preferred my brother to me because he continued to swing him. I began to feel insecure in my value; an uncertainty about my dad took root and was to influence our future relationship. We didn't know how to relate to each other. We had nothing in common, and the differences between us led me to believe that a relationship with this man could not happen and that he wasn't interested in me.

As time passed, a number of things happened for my dad that meant some changes took place, and this consequently had an impact on our relationship. We moved to a house which was near a river; Dad had a work colleague who was a boat fanatic, and this had whet his appetite for the love of boats. Not long after that, my great-nan died and left Dad some money which meant he was able to buy himself a boat. But instead of buying the boat, he decided to make it from a kit. He told me that it was cheaper to buy a kit than a ready-made boat; it meant he got a good model at less cost! He embraced the challenge to build it despite being teased with jokes of Noah and the ark. He pressed on and was victorious – his 'miracle dinghy' was completed. This brought with it the possibility for my dad and me to make a good connection. I was fascinated with the process of boat-making, and as it began to take shape in our garage, I would go and check out the progress. When the boat was finished, we took it down to the river and set sail. I loved it! I hoped that I would be able to serve a purpose and a sense of value to my dad. However, my joy was short-lived as his job changed, and we had to move house to an area without a river. This meant my dad would have very little time for me or the luxury of sailing any more.

By the time I reached my teenage years, my relationship with my dad had largely broken down, and we only communicated when it was necessary. I continued to live out the lie that I was of no value to him. The indifference between us began to feed my negativity towards him. By this time, my dad was a church minister and a leader in a growing church. He was highly respected. People used to say to me, 'Your dad is so lovely, isn't he?' I would think, 'Really? Why don't I see that?' It made me angry that his church would see this side to him, but I never did. I felt he was aloof towards me, and I was fast losing respect for him. It seemed anything he did have to say to me was negative or corrective, so I thought it pointless to even try to have a relationship with him. I couldn't see what I'd done to deserve this treatment. I spent hours and hours on my own. My bedroom was my safe haven – a place where I created a nurturing environment for many hamsters over the years. I found purpose in loving them, and they satisfied my need to be needed. I decided that Dad could lead his life, and I would lead mine. This pattern of behaviours and emotions continued until, one day, it all changed.

I was going about my business when Dad called me into his office. He asked me to come and look at something for him. I couldn't believe it! Dad actually wanted my opinion. This moment was the key to a new beginning for us. I felt valued.

The other male role model in my life was my brother, whom I had never learnt how to connect well with. He had a unique way of 'doing' life and it was entirely different to mine. We had little in common to make connection with, and the one occasion that we did, we got into real trouble.

When we were living in the house by the river, we were able to go crabbing off one of the jetties. There were four of us – my brother and his friend Sam, and my friend Victoria and me. First, we visited the local fishmonger to collect our free fish heads and then, armed with our nets, lines and buckets, we headed down to the jetty and hoped the tide would be favourable to us. I loved the freedom we had. I was around 12 years old and my brother was two years younger than me. The river was high and I could see the water breaking as the wind smacked off its surface. I could smell the fresh, earthy dampness of the new tide, and the stagnant, rotten smell of low tide had been blown away. I could hear the jingling sound of wires hitting their masts from the park of dinghies across the way. I felt alive and at home. We were in high spirits, exhilarated with freedom and life. As we reached the jetty, we threw down our stuff, each of us eager to be the one to catch the first crab. The smell of fish filled my nostrils as we pierced the heads with the hooks of our crab lines, and tension filled the atmosphere as the competition began. Within half an hour my brother was the winner, but we all caught our fair share of the ten-legged creatures. It wasn't long before we started to get bored and began to seek out our next adrenaline fix.

It was decided we would head back into town, find the toy shop and see how many things we could steal without being caught. Blinded by competition and fuelled by adrenaline, we reached our destination and entered the shop. We separated out and sought to fulfil our mission. I picked up some stink bombs and a toy monkey. It was sucking its thumb and I thought it was cute. I slipped it inside my clothes. I walked out of the shop with the goods, as well as a guilty conscience. I reconvened with the others a few shops down to swap stories of our trophies. I knew I had done something wrong, and I felt uncomfortable. I'd got away with it for now, but what if I were to be found out? I wasn't keen on the outcome of that, but I showed the others what I'd taken and felt quite pleased with my new monkey. The others were pleased with the stink bombs I had taken and were eager to try them out. I was only too happy to be parted with something that linked me to my crime, so I handed them out.

We began to walk again, with no real destination this time, but with the aim of throwing the stink bombs and watching for reactions when the smell was released. As we were walking, I spotted a lady with dwarfism and decided she could be the target of my stink bomb. I positioned myself to throw and then hide so I could watch for her reaction. To my dismay, the bomb landed just behind her and she walked on unaware of the smell that filled the air in her wake. Looking back, I am grateful for that.

Just a few days later, we decided we would attempt more shoplifting at the toy store, following our recent success. The feelings of guilt had shifted and I felt liberated by the power I had. I was bolder than before and felt I could manage a few more things this time, and once again, I left the shop with goods that didn't belong to me. I didn't feel as guilty this time. This was something I was good at.

Some time had passed and Mum and Dad planned to take my brother and I out to buy new decorations for our rooms. We had moved into a house that was very rundown and lots of work had been going on to make it more homely. It was our turn now, and we were looking forward to it. Family days out did not happen often – we usually argued about our destination and could never seem to agree on anything, but today was scheduled to be a good day, and we were in good spirits.

As we finished breakfast, Dad announced that on our way, we would be going to thank Victoria's mum for the gifts she had bought us recently. He left the table and walked out of the room. My heart sank and began to beat faster. We had told Mum and Dad that the things we had stolen had come from Victoria's mum as gifts. Now we had a choice: we could face Victoria's mum or we could own up to what we had done and face the consequences. We didn't feel we could own up to everything, so we told them that we had stolen some of the items and, not thinking it through, we said we had stolen the money from Victoria's mum. Obviously, we now had to face the consequences for our actions, so it was just a matter of what that would be. My brother and I waited in the kitchen for the verdict. Mum and Dad came back with a number of consequences.

They decided that we would each spend the day in our rooms rather than going out, but before that, we were escorted back to the shop with the items we had taken. Dad told me that I was to say sorry to the shopkeeper for stealing and to hand back the things I had taken. Shamefaced, I did as I was instructed and was warned that the police would be involved if I ever tried anything like that again, but I was shown mercy on this occasion. I hadn't come clean about everything, and while Dad spared me the embarrassment of meeting Victoria's mum, I was left to live with guilt because of my dishonesty. The experience did teach me not to lie and steal!

My relationship with my brother had a heavy competitive flavour and I found myself competing with him for our parents' attention. I regularly scrutinized whether their treatment of me, in comparison to my brother, was 'fair' and I usually concluded that it wasn't. Whenever there was a dispute, it felt like I was to blame because I was the eldest. I felt as if I was insignificant and embraced this as being true. I thought I had to seek constant approval of my value to the family, which I'm not sure I found. By the time I was a teenager, as I have mentioned earlier, I had established a pattern of retreating to my room and learnt how to enjoy my own company, rather than working out how I could feel connected. I saw my brother as an enemy, but instead of putting up a fight, I decided to opt out and chose isolation and independence. We didn't talk much, until we had grown up and had families of our own.

Given the relationships I had with my dad and brother, I couldn't help wondering what was going to happen when my son was born. How would I respond to him? How would he respond to me? Would I be a fair mother to a girl and boy? Would I favour Zoe over Daniel?

I have always had a determined spirit, so I made the decision that I was going to make this work. I knew I could do it. I could fix and change my belief system. Daniel, along with Andy, could heal my emotions. I was ready. Daniel's arrival was fast approaching and I felt so satisfied. I thought I was sorted. I had a lovely husband and was soon to have two children, a girl and a boy. Life was perfect!

This perfect life was about to come crashing down around me.

6

Daniel

At thirty-seven weeks and five days pregnant, I was not feeling good and was up more than usual in the night. At 5 a.m. I woke again, placed my hands over my swollen abdomen and pressed my fingers in to disturb my little boy, just to check he was OK. He responded by nudging me back. Reassured, I went back to sleep.

When I woke later, I was aware something wasn't right. I felt odd and Daniel's position was making me feel uncomfortable. Feeling anxious, I got into the shower; that usually made him wriggle, but not this time. His foot was wedged under one of my ribs like a pole holding up a washing line. Adrenalin was coursing through my veins, causing sweat beads to form on my freshly washed body. I was scared. I needed to get myself checked and Andy had left for work already, so I rang his mum, and told her I was worried and asked her if she could look after Zoe so that I could go to the hospital.

With my heart in my mouth, I drove the eight minutes to the pregnancy Day Assessment Unit at the local hospital. It was already bustling with women, all at various stages of pregnancy, and the day had barely begun! I gave the receptionist my name and said that I needed to get my baby checked as I hadn't felt him move this morning.

I sat down and waited my turn and wondered why they were showing no sense of urgency. The fear within me was growing, my heart was pounding and my palms were sweaty. I was dealing with the emotional tussle of wanting to prolong time in order to avoid hearing the words I so dreaded, 'Your baby has died,' and the alternative of being seen quickly to put me out of my misery. I longed to be told, 'All is well.' As I waited, I was distracted from the torture in my head by the conversations the other mums were having.

I don't remember how long I sat there listening and watching, but my turn eventually came. The room I entered was light, the window frame stretched from one side of the room to the other. Outside, the world was going by, while mine had come to a screaming halt. Under the window was a bed that was hard, cold and square. It was solid enough to take the weight of a heavily expectant mother and hold the mystery of life unseen. The whitewashed walls were adorned with posters of the pregnant mother, cross sections of foetal positions and checklists for midwives to follow. Medical equipment was hanging around as if waiting for a time to become useful, waiting and listening to the intimate details of each story being told. My mystery was about to be unveiled.

A kind-faced midwife entered the room and I had her attention. As I lay on the bed, she listened to my concerns. Then she picked up a two-ended cone, known as a Pinard horn, which she rested on my bare abdomen and placed her ear to the other end. As she listened, I was frozen in position, full of fear and hope. The clock on the wall seemed to tick louder and louder, as though it was mimicking the hope of a beating heart.

The Pinard horn didn't seem to be giving her the information she was looking for, so she gently reassured me that sometimes they miss transmitting the sound of the heartbeat, depending on the baby's position. She left the room and returned with a machine and another midwife. I wondered if I'd manage to carry on breathing in my icy place of time suspension. Deliberately now, I took a new and deep inhalation of air like my life depended on it, and we moved to the next stage of discovery. The midwives rigged me up to the machine. The straps of pink and blue spread across my stomach looking like they were holding cargo in place ready for a long journey. Attached to one of these straps was a round disc which snuggled close to the outside wall of my rounded stomach. Once in place, this disc was able to announce the verdict.

There was no evidence of Daniel's heartbeat coming from this machine. I knew this silence spoke of death. The midwives clearly wanted this to be a different story for me: 'Is there anyone we can call for you?'

Andy was forty-five minutes away and as it happened, my friend Yvonne worked two floors above this room. Anticipating good news of Daniel's arrival, she responded to the midwives' request to come to see me and arrived in the room very quickly. Her bounce was stilled when she saw my face and knew immediately that this was not the good news she was expecting. She knew that I was about to embark on a devastating journey, one which she also had experienced some years earlier. Filled with empathy, Yvonne came with me as we made our way up in the lift to the top floor for my scan. It felt like I was walking the plank towards news that would swallow me up and drown me. There was still a glimmer of hope, wasn't there? Surely the machine could be wrong?

The windowless room we entered was dim; there was a small lamp on a table which brought light only to that corner. There was an L-shaped medical bed, adorned with a pillow and paper to protect it. This was to give little comfort to me as I climbed on and got into position. The warm gel and scanning wand was placed upon my abdomen and transmitted the news to the screen. Moments like this frame time. Time stops.

With a serious face, the sonographer turned to me and said, 'I am really sorry, your baby has died.' Daniel's heart was no longer beating and this was the end of his journey. He was gone.

In the stillness, I began to absorb the news and realized I needed to tell Andy. I wondered how he would react. How would he cope? Reality started to dawn on me. I would need to share our story and face the sea of expectant people who had been waiting to rejoice with us. Now they would be drawn into the sadness and heartache with us.

I am a practical person and it wasn't long before I thought about what I had to do with the immediate situation. I had to give birth to a dead baby. Frozen with fear and dread, Yvonne supported me, and guided me to another quiet room for space to think and reflect.

The next thing I needed to do was to tell Andy that his precious little son had died. On the table before me was a phone which I could use to contact him. Armed with a number, I got through to him and announced the words no father ever wants to hear. It's awful telling news like that over the phone, but there was no use in lying or hiding anything. I needed him to come and be with me, and he would need a good reason to leave work at that time.

Forty minutes later, Andy joined me and I thanked Yvonne for all her kind support. I was so grateful to her for being there for me in my moment of need. She was a rock and I'll never forget her kindness. She slipped out of the room and went back to work. Andy and I embraced each other, words failed us and grief blanketed the moment. This blanket, however, provided no warmth or protection from the cold. On the contrary, this blanket brought with it an icy exposure to the loss that was about to shape our world. Our tears began to flow for the present and for the future, our emotions spilling over for the loss and pain that had just entered our lives.

Time lapsed and my practical mind began to emerge once more. While part of me was captured by emotions that couldn't escape the jaws of death, I was also aware that I had a physical job to do. Labour and birth. A gruelling job which wouldn't yield a reward, as it had done with Zoe. I wondered if I could be saved from this ordeal. Maybe I could have a caesarean and bypass the pain of labour and the trauma of pushing? The pushing part was what I dreaded the most. I prayed, 'Please, God, take that from me, I don't think I can handle it. Is it not enough that I've toiled through the pregnancy and endured the pain of an unstable pelvis for months and all for nothing? No gift, no joy. Just emptiness.'

The doctors came to see us and we were asked if we would like to go home and come back tomorrow, or go and get some clothes and essentials and come back later. I was very clear about one thing. I knew I needed Daniel out of my body. I was freaked out about the whole thing. I needed him out as soon as possible. Coming back tomorrow was an even worse thought than knowing Daniel was dead inside me. I did need to collect some belongings, so we made our way back home.

There was no need for questions; our tear-stained faces told our news. Shock rippled the atmosphere. No one spoke, our emotions were shared in silence. There were no words, apart from those to organize for Zoe to stay at Grandma and Grandpa's house. With a heavy heart, I climbed the stairs to our bedroom to get my labour bag.

Every room tells a story. In contrast to the functional medical rooms that we had just vacated, our bedroom represented a safe haven where love dwelt. The sloping roofs and floral print wallpaper gave the room a comforting feeling. As I entered the room, I stood poised. I absorbed the panoramic view of a room which spoke of happiness and anticipation. Preparations for Daniel's arrival had commenced and his cot stood at the side of the room. Piled into it were a Moses basket and nappy-changing mat. It was like a pile of presents waiting for an excited child to open them. It's funny how your emotions can change towards possessions. Only yesterday, I had felt excited and full of hope towards these objects. Today, these items felt cruel and taunting to my pregnant frame. They were of no use to me now. They pointed out the hard reality of a hope stolen. I hoped they would be removed from here by the time I returned empty-handed.

My thoughts moved on to my parents and how I might make contact with them. They were on holiday in Skiathos, a Greek island. I knew the holiday tour company name, so that was a place to start. I picked up the phone and rang our church minister, who took the task of locating my parents to give them the news. I also rang my friend Julie and her husband, Simon. We asked them if they could spread the news to our friends. The grapevine could do the rest of the work, so I didn't need to keep going over the story and support the listener in coping with my bad news. I grabbed the labour bag, which had been kitted out with clothes, toiletries and a camera. We said our goodbyes to Zoe and Andy's mum and headed back to the hospital labour ward.

We entered the ward and were greeted by Nicholas. He grinned on seeing us and in a humorous (and rather loud) voice said, 'Hello, the lovely Mr and Mrs Rutland, is your baby about to join us?' He reached out to shake Andy's hand, clearly unaware of our position. Nicholas was my appointed midwife and we had got to know him as our friend. I had met him at antenatal classes during my pregnancy with Zoe and in the last few months, Andy and I had got to know him better while doing mime tours. For some years, both Andy and I had been involved with a Christian mime troupe. We'd travelled around local Salvation Army corps and performed mimes to music. Nicholas had joined us recently on our travels and supported the team with sound and lights.

Our response to his greeting alerted Nicholas that all was not well. He became serious and resolved to take us under his wing and have full responsibility for our care. He was able to hand over his current clients and he became designated solely to us. It was good for Andy and me to have a familiar face looking after us. I felt we had been provided for.

As we walked onto the labour ward, we were shown to a room which was large and airy and had its own toilet and shower. This was to be our room for as long as we needed. The room was at the end of the ward, so it was sheltered from the sound of other babies entering the world. This cry was a sound I longed to hear but knew that what I was going to hear was silence. The cries of other babies would have tormented me.

Before the hospital staff could induce labour, I needed to be checked out medically. A male doctor took a number of vials of blood to send off for testing and I pleaded with him, 'Please can I have a caesarean?' His explanation was not one I wanted to hear, 'This would not be a good option for you. There are risks with surgery and you will recover better, emotionally and physically, if you do this naturally.' I had no choice but to go through with this. My world had been turned upside down and I felt sick to my toes, but I just needed to go with it and not fight against the system.

My induction was successful and within a few hours I was in established labour. Contractions came on my body like waves on the shore, each one intense and intentional. I gripped the gas and air mouthpiece and inhaled deep breaths. It had a soaking effect that spread through my body. It seemed to take me somewhere else, like I was in the room, but not in myself. It numbed the physical and emotional pain that I was experiencing. For the time being, at least.

Sometime during all of this, my consultant came in to see me. She was an authoritative woman who held command over her patients and staff. She wore a smart suit and had brown hair shaped in a bob. She spoke of how sorry she was that this had happened and explained that medically they had done all they could to care for me. 'Well, that's good for you, but that doesn't help me right now,' I thought. I wanted her to go away. I shut my eyes. I didn't want to engage in conversation on this level. I was now gripped with physical pain every few moments and all I wanted to know was when I could have an epidural. It all felt unfair, cruel and so pointless. She told me they were waiting on blood results to check if it was safe to proceed with an epidural. I wished they would be quicker! The pain intensity was increasing with each contraction, my whole body roaring like a tormented lion. This was not fair!

My bloods eventually came back, allowing me to have the epidural and once it was up and running, I felt a little more settled. Now we were playing a waiting game – waiting for my body to be ready and in position for Daniel's delivery. The contractions continued to do their worst but the pain was masked by the drugs going into my spine.

Time moved on and my body prepared for delivery. The dreaded moment had arrived. Andy and Nicholas had been chatting quietly about the music they liked, while I lay with my eyes closed wishing I wasn't there. I sat forward slightly to let Nicholas know that although I was without pain, I felt a sensation that made me think Daniel was about to enter the world. I was right and Daniel's head came out without even a shove from me. Nicholas assisted with the rest of the delivery. All I needed to give was one little push. I had done it.

It was a strange moment with mixed emotions. I had survived the ordeal of childbirth, which was great, but my baby was lying dead in front of me. I had loved and nurtured him for the past nine months and the fact he was dead didn't change my desire to know all about him. I wanted to know what he looked like. What colour was his hair and how much did he have? How big was he? Did he look like me or Andy? His limp and lifeless body granted the answers to the questions that I'd longed to know since I knew of his existence.

My emotions were torn. I wanted him. I wanted to cuddle him, kiss him, dress him, feed him and love him. I wanted to keep him, but I knew he was not mine to keep now. His body would decay and his life was gone. I could have had as much time with him as I had wanted. I could have bathed and dressed him, but it seemed like pretending. I didn't want to play a game – like those days of playing dolls as a girl. He wouldn't have known my love. He was gone. I couldn't do it. Nicholas dressed Daniel in a nappy and a pale blue Babygro which had a little motif of a teddy on the upper left chest. He wrapped him in a blanket and handed him to me. I held my baby son. His eyes were closed and unaware of what his existence meant to us. His 8lb 1oz weight, dead in my arms.

I tried to glean as much detail about him as I could. He had a dimple on his chin, just like his dad, sister and grandma. He had a smattering of dark hair and a stubby nose. His fingers were chubby. I held him for a short while, as Andy looked on.

We exchanged looks through glazed eyes. In total silence and without any words, we acknowledged the hopes and dreams that we'd had for our son were over before they had begun. Andy took Daniel from me and as he cradled his precious son in his arms, the tears rolled down his cheeks.

Too numb and shocked for tears, I accepted that this was how it was. My role as a mother to my son ended here and as hard as that was to accept, that was a fact. I knew I may never discover the mother/son relationship which I had prepared myself for, but I had no choice other than to live with that too.

After we had held our son, we placed him in a cot behind one of the privacy hospital curtains in the room. Nicholas asked whether we wanted to keep him with us or whether he should send a porter to collect Daniel to take him to the mortuary. I didn't really want him in the room, but I wasn't quite ready to let him go either. It was decided to put him in the room opposite ours that was rarely used, other than for storage. This is where he stayed for the night.

My night was long and dark. The bustle of movement beyond our closed door was the only evidence I had that the world still carried on. I heard the distant cry of a newborn baby that made my heart ache. It was a sound I would never hear from Daniel. Even his sleep was silent. I felt nauseous and my insides felt so tight I thought they might crush me. Andy, in the bed beside me, was quiet. I didn't feel I had anything to say either. I don't know if he was awake or asleep and I couldn't be bothered to ask. I was holding my emotions like a canal lock that is full to the brim, its stone walls and wooden gates holding the weight of water in its tank. The night was locked in. I lay there, barely moving, afraid to let my tears out in case I would be unable to stop them.

Dawn arrived and brought with it a new day. The wooden gates which had been holding my tears crept open against my will and I began to sob. I shook and I didn't know what to do with myself. The roaring sound of grief was overwhelming. A nauseous yearning, a heaviness deep within me took residence in my being. It was uninvited but it had come to stay for what seemed like forever.

Daniel lay silent in the room opposite. He wasn't far away. My tears paused, and as I went through the motions of getting myself washed and dressed, I felt numb and locked down. Andy was with me and going through his own nightmare of emotions. We couldn't cancel out each other's pain, and neither of us could avoid walking along the path, deep in the valley in which we found ourselves. In turmoil and not yet ready to leave our son, we remained on the ward. I was longing for Daniel and missing Zoe, so we asked if Andy's mum could bring her to us. At some point that morning, they arrived along with the minister of our church.

I wrapped my arms around Zoe, breathing in her life, her warmth, her smell and received the love she offered. At 21 months, she had little understanding of what was going on, but pointed to my tummy button and said, 'Daniel?' Tears exposed the truth and they streamed down my cheeks. My precious daughter was so young, how was I to explain this situation to her? She turned her face towards mine in search for her answer and on seeing my tears she simply said, 'Tears. Mummy, hug.'

My heart was broken, shattered into tiny pieces. I couldn't find the words, they were scattered and unconnected all over my brain. Where were the words I needed? Zoe didn't understand the word 'death', or even 'life'. She may have thought 'Daniel' was the name for a 'belly button', and she certainly wouldn't have understood why both Mummy and Daddy were crying. I needed her to see Daniel, I needed to capture a mental picture of us as a family. No one could take the memory of us all being together, even if that was all I could take away with me. I needed to tell Zoe that Daniel was her brother, that he was a baby, not a belly button!

Andy and I gathered Zoe in our arms and went into the room where Daniel lay. It was large, airy and full of medical equipment – not unlike the room we had come from. Daniel was lying in one of the plastic basin cots and we showed him to Zoe. We told her that this was her brother, but we couldn't keep him because he had died. Zoe seemed to accept this and said, 'Daniel.' We all said goodbye to him and left the room. The picture of the four of us together will remain in my memory forever.

Leaving the hospital without our precious son was excruciating. We caught glimpses of other parents on their way home with their new bundles of joy and it highlighted our loss.

At that moment, life seemed so unfair.

7

Rainbows

Once at home, I thought I could try to hide from the world – perhaps I could pretend that time had stopped. This, of course, was wishful thinking as there was no stopping for Zoe! There was a life to be lived, and in many ways, she was our lifesaver and reason to carry on living. We were still Mummy and Daddy, and this was something for which we were so thankful.

It was day three after giving birth to Daniel which was the most difficult time for me. Day three, following a birth is notoriously written about. Milk comes into the breasts and 'baby blues' hormones can make you tearful. I was well-endowed in the breast department so when my milk came in, it was excruciating. My breasts were as large as two watermelons and felt just as hard. I experienced the pains and the increase in size and yet I had no baby to feed. This upset me more than I can describe. I had no control over my body's response. It was cruel, and I wanted my baby back.

Four days after Daniel was born, we were able to arrange for his funeral to take place. It was a simple affair. Andy and I, our parents and the minister and his wife were the only ones there. I didn't want to engage in conversation with anyone. The thing that I found with grief was that when I shared about my loss,

I found myself supporting the other person. I had taken on a sense of responsibility for the emotions of other people, and I felt that if I dumped my sadness in their lap, they may not know what to do with it. I felt I needed to help them, to give them my listening ear and tell them it was not as bad as they might think. This reaction took enormous effort and in time I learnt how to do it, but for the time being, avoidance was my chosen option and my son's funeral was a very private occasion.

Daniel's tiny wooden coffin arrived at the crematorium on the back seat of a Volvo. On top of it, we had laid a single white rose. It was weird to think that our son lay in that box. Saying goodbye to him was a spiritual experience for me; I was there present in the room and yet I also felt like I was somewhere else – the occasion held something of a picture that was bigger than me. I had never lost anybody close to me before. After the short service, I stood by the coffin. I had intended to say my final goodbye, in order to begin the process of closure. As I stood there, a wave of peace began to fill my insides and I had a clear sense that this separation was temporary. I was filled with hope. This may seem strange, as we see death as being so final. The person we know and love is here no more. Their body has gone. Then, these words entered my mind: 'You'll be with him again one day, this is temporary.' I left Daniel there and said to myself, 'Bye for now, son, see you again someday.' Softening the edges of finality made the whole experience more bearable. That's not to say it made it all better – it didn't! I simply felt strong enough to walk away.

It took a long time to recover from this loss. I would think of Daniel every moment of every day. I physically ached for him and I wondered when the intensity of pain and yearning would lessen. I found solace in reading novels in order to take a break from reality. Months went by and still the pain remained.

Three months had passed when I discovered I was pregnant again. Once again, I had some hope. But this hope was short-lived, as I started to bleed. My hope was gone and my dreams were shattered once again.

My emotions spiralled downward and I began to lose my sense of reality. I started to believe that everything that was good about my life had gone bad. I wanted to die. I played with suicidal thoughts and considered how I might end it all. I thought about the various options but fortunately I never got to the point where I took any action.

I found myself in the company of a kind lady from our church who spent some time with me. She listened to me, guided me and empathized with me through her own experience of loss. She related to me with gentleness as she reflected that her world had been rocked too, when she had lost her husband and was left with two small children to raise alone. She shared how she'd got through and survived, and her strength and determination was the inspiration I needed. From this point, I was able to pick myself up, brush myself down and pull myself away from self-pity. I had my life ahead of me, full of purpose and opportunity. My husband and daughter needed me and wanted me to stick around.

The intensity of loss was a paralysing experience that hung around like a bad smell. It was all-consuming, but its pungency was diluted by the passage of time, and after a while, I didn't notice it so powerfully. Grief was like that. At the beginning, I thought of Daniel every moment of every day. After a while, this turned into some moments of every day, then to one moment every day and to a few moments in a week and so on. Each thought was attached to an emotion but as time went on, the thoughts lessened and the emotions lost some of their intensity. Part of the healing process for me, was being able to have another baby. I knew no one could ever replace Daniel, but my maternal instinct needed satiating. I hoped another baby would satisfy this craving and aid me in my journey of recovery.

Seven months after losing Daniel, I became pregnant again. My fifth positive pregnancy test and one living child to show for it. I hoped against hope that this pregnancy would bring me another child who would live. From this place of hope, I prayed to God, 'Will you give me a guarantee that my baby won't die?' To be honest, I didn't really expect an answer. I did believe God had helped me from a distance, but I'd seen little measurable outcome so far. How surprised was I when a lady came up to me the following Sunday – not knowing I was pregnant again – and said she felt God wanted to show me a psalm: 'Take delight in the Lord, and he will give you the desires of your heart' (Ps. 37:4).

Had my prayer been answered? If it had, the desire of my heart was to have a living baby at the end of my pregnancy, so I had to ask myself, was I delighting in the Lord? I remembered attending an evening service about a week after Daniel was born and throwing my hands in the air in worship because I didn't know what else to do with myself. I had felt at the mercy of God and I knew he was way bigger than I could ever fully understand.

I struggled to know what delighting in the Lord really meant. Did I get great pleasure from God? Did I rejoice or praise him? I wondered if it was necessary or even possible for me to do a deal with God. Perhaps if I made it my business to praise him, then maybe he would give me a living baby? I'm not sure how, or if, God measures praise or makes deals with people, but I knew I was grateful to him for giving me my husband and daughter and my friends and family. I knew I was grateful for the strength and support he had given me when I lost Daniel, especially as I did not have to push. I felt he had carried me when my next pregnancy had failed, by giving me a friend who could empathize with me. I knew I was grateful that Andy had a job, and for our lovely home. Somehow, I was able to see this provision as being from God, but to praise and delight in him in light of what had just happened to me? I wasn't sure, but I was willing to try.

I chose to believe these words had been an answer to my prayer; I felt uplifted. I had met hope and it was a far better companion than fear. But fear was persistent, it pestered me and prodded me. It taunted me and told me that I was deluded to think I had heard from God. Fear would not leave me alone. I tried to tell it to go away, and it did for a while, but then it came back again. There were times when it took all my effort to choose to hope. It may seem obvious to choose hope over fear, but it took a huge amount of strength and determination. Hope was something that filled me with the anticipation that something good might happen, but it held no guarantees. Hope did not expect me to blindly believe, but it pointed me in the direction of joy.

Perhaps because hope brings no guarantees, there is nothing solid for it to stick to. When it's gone, what's left? Nothing. The absence of hope can leave a vulnerable empty space, and that empty space can be filled with fear.

I searched for hope. I used all the strength and determination I had, but I continued to battle with fear. It was exhausting. Nine months is a long time to wait when you want something so desperately. When I was tired, fear was at its strongest. When I was about thirty weeks pregnant, I once again found myself frantic with fear and desperate for hope, so I cried out to God, 'Please give me a guarantee that my baby won't die. I know it's a lot to ask – you're out there, busy with everyone else's lives and I'm only me and I know you gave me that verse but, please, I'm desperate.'

When I woke up the next day, a picture of a rainbow came to my mind. Rainbows signify promise to me. There's a well-known story in the book of Genesis about Noah, who had built an ark. The floods came and after they had dried out, God placed a rainbow before Noah and said, 'I promise I will never flood the entire earth again.' So, with this picture in my mind I asked, 'Can you give me a rainbow to show that you promise you won't let this happen again?' Within moments of my prayer, Zoe called out to me, 'Can I get out of bed now, Mummy?' She came in holding an open hardback book. I couldn't believe my eyes; there was a rainbow stretched out across the two pages! Zoe had selected it from a collection of other books in her room. I hadn't seen this one in a while and it wasn't one of her favourites. This just happened to be the one she chose for today! I felt excited and hopeful once more. I was grateful to God for being there for me and answering my prayer. I began to believe that I mattered to him.

When Andy came in from work that evening, I couldn't wait to tell him about what had happened with the rainbow. But before I could get to the bit about Zoe coming in with the book, he jumped in and said, 'Did you see it, then?'

'If you let me finish, I'll get to that bit!'

He, now also excited, said, 'There was one in the sky as I was driving to work. Did you see it too?'

Our desire for a living baby became more than hope at this point. It was the beginning of certainty. We chose to see something of God that was bigger than us, rather than just assuming the moment was a coincidence. Hope was now joined with faith. We didn't create it, earn it or even understand it, but we knew it was with us. It was a gift. Something supernatural had occurred. My hope became more solid, more resistant to fear and I felt stronger to face my niggling doubts.

The following week, we saw another rainbow. After that, we saw another and then another and another! Throughout the final months of my pregnancy, September and October 1999, Andy and I witnessed more rainbows than I've ever seen in my life! I was awestruck and these rainbows fuelled my faith. I knew that this was going to be OK. Sure enough, Georgia Lucy Rutland's arrival was marked by a massive rainbow outside the labour room window. She was healthy and, despite a traumatic delivery, both Georgia and I were alive.

The mixture of joy and relief that I felt gave way to gratitude and an abundance of happy tears. I didn't mind being an emotional wreck this time. Georgia's little face was perfect, her heart was beating and her chest rose and fell as she breathed in the air of life. My rainbow baby had arrived, and what an emotional rollercoaster ride we had travelled. Georgia's birth was like a mountaintop experience in which I glanced heavenwards with gratitude and acknowledged my humanity and vulnerability. Having God involved opened up a whole new dimension which blew my mind and helped me greatly. I expressed my deep thankfulness to God for the gift of her life and his faithfulness in delivering his promise.

My mum and dad brought Zoe in to meet Georgia. They told us that in the lift on the way up, Zoe had told someone, 'I'm going to see my baby sister and she's alive!' I felt like heaven had just touched earth. I wanted this feeling to stay forever; I wanted to hold on to it and not let it go. The richness of joy was a treasure. It was like holding golden sand in my hands – it sparkled and flowed with no edges or boundaries as it filtered through my fingers, tangible but not containable.

This moment was a gift. I was submerged in joy, and it was liberating and healing to my wounded soul.

For a couple of weeks following Georgia's birth, I experienced waves of joy and tiredness. I was so grateful for my two demanding little girls, but found I needed to balance things very carefully. Zoe was very intense with Georgia and, at 3 years old, wasn't old enough to understand how to handle a newborn baby, even though she believed she could. My heart skipped a beat or two when Zoe picked up her baby sister and carried her around!

Luckily, Georgia was an easy baby. She would feed and then sleep for three hours, and then be ready for the next feed. It would take fifteen minutes for her to fill up, I'd change her, then she'd go back to sleep. I couldn't quite believe how stress-free she was and I loved cuddling her. She was a true blessing following the long pregnancy and losing Daniel.

At 22 days old, Georgia slept through the night and I couldn't believe how amazing she was. However, one night when I went to check on her, I realized all was not as it should be. I began to gather her in my arms and she screamed out. Georgia's normal cry was so soft and gentle and this pitched scream was not the sound I recognized. I knew instantly something was wrong. Her body was hot in my hands and alarm bells began to ring loudly in my ears.

Anxious and concerned, I called for help.

8

Hospitals and Health

By the end of that day, Georgia had been admitted to hospital. I was scared and fraught. She had undergone various tests, including a lumbar puncture to check for meningitis, as her temperature was unusually high for a newborn baby. We had no idea what was wrong with her. She screamed whenever anyone touched her. She was put on IV fluids and antibiotics and we were told that time would tell if she would improve or not.

Once again, I was filled with fear. I asked the doctors if she was going to die. I was sure I wouldn't survive that tragedy. After three days of limited handling and small amounts of milk, much to my relief, Georgia improved. She began feeding properly again and tolerated me holding her without screaming, so it was agreed that we could go home. Panic over!

Life with a 3-year-old and a newborn settled once again and we all fell into a routine. Zoe was going to nursery a few times a week and I treasured my time with Georgia. But three weeks later, Georgia got ill again. She had bronchiolitis which meant she needed to be admitted to hospital for antibiotics and oxygen therapy. Once more, her feeding pattern shifted and my milk production reduced significantly. I couldn't believe we were here again! My baby girl struggled to breathe and coughed and coughed. The bronchiolitis virus caused white stickiness to cover the small air sacs which compromised her oxygen exchange. This time, I just went with the process. I knew about bronchiolitis and how it worked and I had a feeling it would all be OK. That doesn't mean I found it easy. I missed Zoe and Andy. I wanted to be able to enjoy my family in the comfort of my home. However, time soon passed and we were homeward-bound once again.

This time, we enjoyed six weeks of family time before Georgia got sick again. She was so hot and at one time her temperature went as high as 42°C, or 107.6°F. At one point, she became floppy as her temperature peaked. I tried to cool her with a wet flannel – paracetamol and ibuprofen weren't shifting the heat. I was worried, and needed some answers as to why this was happening.

At paediatric A & E, they managed to get a urine sample which showed lots of bugs. Yet again, Georgia had a cannula inserted into her veins to administer IV antibiotics and she was admitted for treatment. The children's ward was quite familiar to me now and we settled into the cubicle with resigned sighs. The staff welcomed us back which took some of the edge of disappointment away. The doctors informed me that it was unusual for a 3-month-old infant to get a urine infection so they would do some investigations to find out why.

We stayed in a few days and, during this time, an ultrasound test showed us that Georgia had a duplex kidney which meant that one of her kidneys was bigger than the other. This wasn't the reason why she had got the infection and it fortunately posed no increased risk or problem to her then or in the future. We had no further occurrences of infection. I was grateful to be able to go home and get on with enjoying my family. Georgia was a delightful baby and toddler. She hit all her milestones within normal boundaries. She was laid-back and fitted in with family demands. I felt so blessed.

Throughout January 2001, Zoe had several high temperatures with unknown origins that lasted around ten days each time, and these caused me some concern. Then, over the next couple of months, her weight began to drop. By March it was clear that it was quite low for her 4-and-a-half years, and I knew something was not right. It all became very clear one Saturday at the end of March.

Zoe began the day being incredibly thirsty. She would finish one drink and then request another. I thought this a bit odd, as drinking was something I always had to encourage her to do. Towards the end of the afternoon my brain was highly stimulated. Zoe had continued her extreme thirst all day, and my suspicions of Type 1 diabetes had gone into overdrive. The adrenalin available to me, an anxious parent, pricked the inside of my skin and I felt uncomfortable. I drew on memories from my nurse training about detection of diabetes. I recalled the history of diabetes and how, in the eighteenth century, tasting urine to check for sweetness was a way of establishing the presence of diabetes.

A mother's love for her child knows no bounds! Plus, I was impatient – I didn't want to wait for a formal diagnosis knowing what I knew. Zoe's limitless thirst meant that she needed to pee every half hour or so. It was after one of these visits, I noticed a drip of wee on the seat of the toilet. I can't believe I did it but I dipped the very tip of my finger into that drip and placed it on the tip of my tongue. A sweetness hit my taste buds. That was my answer, diagnosed there and then. Zoe had diabetes. The adrenalin that had been trickling under my skin began to rush. It was like a motorway of traffic had joined my blood capillaries – busy, fast-moving and heavy. Our journey was about to take another direction and I didn't want to go that way, but I wasn't in control. Life had a funny way of sweeping me along. I felt as though I had missed the turning and was being ushered into the rush of fast-moving traffic. Zoe was admitted to hospital.

The day was drawing to a close as we settled onto the ward and Zoe was given her first, tiny dose of insulin to bring her blood sugars down a bit. It was a blessing she was so accepting about being injected and having her finger pricked for blood testing. We had been given a room to ourselves and once Zoe had gone to sleep, I had some space to think. I couldn't believe it. I would never have thought that my nursing experience would be something I would need to use for personal reasons. I recalled the teaching package I had created in my training. At least this was something I didn't need to learn, and I could concentrate on how to administer Zoe's insulin and dietary intake and deal with our emotions about the whole thing.

Life was full of challenges and I'd realized by now that I couldn't choose to avoid them. The choice I did have, however, was how I would respond to what had come my way. This was a moment when I realized I needed to choose joy, even though the situation didn't lend itself to that. My experiences so far had taught me to look for the positives, but all of this was still pushing my boundaries. It was one thing to lose my son and have a rocky beginning for Georgia, but not this as well. Positivity was hard to grapple with.

Emotions aside, I had some practicalities to take on board. Despite the fact that Zoe was sleeping soundly, her blood sugars needed to be checked to see what the insulin had done. This was the first of many nights of broken sleep in order to keep Zoe's blood sugar levels safe. The wonders of technology helped to show us if the insulin had dropped her sugars too low.

Even if I was gentle waking Zoe, it seemed cruel to demand that she drink sugary milk and insist that she eat a digestive biscuit, but it was important that we brought her blood sugar levels up to safe levels. I hated this scenario which we revisited many, many times over the years. Sometimes, Zoe would sit up as requested and with her eyes still closed, slurp and crunch and return to her slumber position, and sometimes she would refuse, cry, properly wake herself up and protest again. On these occasions the gentle approach of waking her would often end with cross words and threats if she didn't drink and eat. I found these times so hard, but we had no option but to work with it, and compliance was imperative or Zoe was in serious medical danger. I felt the pain of being a parent in these times and maybe this was when I learnt what 'tough love' was. I had to upset my precious child for her good – pushed into an uncompromising situation with my sole option to choose to accept it or be miserable about it.

I chose to be miserable on countless occasions. I didn't want Zoe to have diabetes. I didn't want to inject her four times a day or jab her finger six or more times a day. She didn't want to have it. Andy didn't want her to have it. None of us wanted it, but here it was. It was an uninvited guest and it was here to stay, like it or lump it, and who in their right mind would like it? So, lump it, it would have to be. Our 'perfect' child was no longer 'perfect', she'd been scarred with a chronic condition and her life would never be the same again. At least our hopes and dreams for her still existed, unlike the ones we had for Daniel, which had no compromise. As I journeyed with the all too familiar grieving process, I realized that as Zoe's mum and role model, it would be my attitude to her diabetes that would determine her outlook. I had a job to do and I needed to be positive for her. I wanted to 'turn our stumbling blocks into stepping stones', not only for Zoe, but for us all.

About six months after Zoe's diagnosis, we went on a diabetes weekend with other families in the same situation as us. We gained knowledge, shared similar experiences and found support. I think it was a little too soon for me to engage in this process, as I found the weekend very stressful and distressing. I'm not sure I'd got to the point of acceptance by then and for any positive point offered, I always had a counteracting argument ready in my head. But I do believe this is where the seed of hope began. That weekend, we heard various speakers share their inspirational stories of what they had achieved despite their diabetes. Managing diabetes and maintaining correct blood sugar levels was a never-ending rollercoaster. Balancing food and insulin was hard, and Zoe's blood sugars rose and fell so dramatically. I didn't understand why I couldn't get it right. The advice from the professionals just didn't seem to work.

Zoe started school in September 2001. Like any other parent, I wanted the best for her and the process of letting go was inevitable. Of course, I missed her, but letting go of the responsibility of monitoring the diabetes was even harder. Her blood sugar control was poor, and not long into the term, I was told her behaviour was not acceptable. I was told she was being spiteful and controlling towards the other children. I felt terrible and somehow responsible for this. Zoe was angry and agitated and I didn't know what to do about it. She was unkind to her peer group and nasty towards Georgia. She did have a lot to contend with, though. Starting school and taking responsibility for her diabetes was a big thing for a little girl who was almost 5 years old. We sought some counselling for Zoe in the hope it would help her to adjust. I think this helped us to understand it better, but her behaviour continued to be a challenge for all of us.

It was also at this time I found out that I was expecting another baby. Tiredness and nausea wasn't a great starting point to the day, and I am sure I could have been more patient with Zoe. I was feeling disappointed that she was being so difficult, so I found it hard to be tolerant with her even though I thought I could understand why.

Time moved on and family life weaved its threads in the great tapestry of life. Zoe and Georgia were their own seamstresses in creating their wishes and desires. My stomach grew slowly this time and the baby's movements were later in gestation than I expected. Life was very full and I was so busy that I chose to spend little time contemplating the possibilities of my pregnancy going wrong again. I was doing daily Heparin injections as I had done with Georgia's pregnancy due to a blood condition that had been discovered after losing Daniel. I saw the professionals as regularly as they had recommended and all my scans were normal. Given the pressures of everyday life, the thought of things not turning out OK only passed through my mind a few times, and I was blessed again with timely rainbows which calmed my fears.

One month before our baby was born, I was given a revelation as to the cause of Zoe's uncontrollable diabetes and behavioural issues. She had complained of earache, so we were at the doctor's to check it out, and while we were waiting, I noticed a large swelling on her neck which turned out to be her thyroid's response to massive amounts of thyroxine. She was diagnosed with Graves' disease for which she had to take tablets. Diagnosis of the Graves' disease highlighted the symptoms Zoe was living with, which would have made her feel terrible for a number of reasons. Her heart was racing, her skin was irritated, her intestines were agitated and her blood sugars needed large doses of insulin to bring them to anywhere near normal results. Her angry, twitchy behaviour wasn't surprising, given all that her body was trying to deal with. She was so aggressive and agitated.

My poor little girl! She'd seen too much of life by the age of just 5. She'd been exposed to the cruelty of nature a number of times and I hadn't been able to protect her from any of it. I believed one of the roles of a mother is to protect from danger and harm. I came to realize that there were limits as to how much I could achieve this. I could see that the diabetes was harming Zoe with waves of blood sugar levels peaking and plunging. It did affect her physical wellbeing for the future as well as in the short term. It felt like giving her insulin and adjusting food intake was somehow protecting her from harm, but it wasn't without cost – like making her eat when she didn't want to.

Her thyrotoxicosis (Graves' disease) harmed her by changing her outward appearance with a massive goitre, it gave her a heart murmur and also affected other people's opinions of her when they observed her agitated behaviour. It also messed around with her diabetes control. I couldn't stop this from hurting her, but I realized I could be part of the solution and this gave me a better outlook. I didn't want to allow myself to be consumed by guilt. I didn't think it would be constructive or helpful to anyone, least of all Zoe. I needed to aim my energies into being the best mum I could be to both Zoe, Georgia and also to the unborn child I was carrying.

I decided to write a journal, to see if I could get clarity and somehow ground the feelings that I was experiencing. I cried out to God to save me from the trap of anxiety and fear. I wrote about how I was relieved that Zoe's behaviour and uncontrollable sugar levels were due to the thyroid, but how sad I was that I had to watch her suffer. I feared for what the future might be for her. As I wrote, I became more aware of my unborn child and what effect my emotions were having on him or her. I began to pray. I asked God for peace and a new perspective. I thanked God for all that I had – for my children and my home, a great medical team and for the rainbows of promise that had carried me through difficult times. Writing this down helped me get some focus. A week passed and I found myself in a different place. Peace had arrived and I was much less anxious.

The day of my planned induction was fast approaching. I had been induced at thirty-seven weeks with Georgia and I was being induced again because of Daniel's stillbirth. I was relieved to not have to go full term, those extra few weeks had held disaster with Daniel and although I had seen the rainbows, I didn't want to test anything! My mum and dad had arrived in order to look after Zoe and Georgia, so Andy and I could go into the hospital to have the baby. We greeted them as usual and Mum handed me a printed bookmark, saying she had seen it and thought of me. On it was a picture of a stone statue of a person embracing a small child, along with the words from Isaiah 41:10, 'fear not, for I am with you, be not dismayed, for I am your God; I will strengthen you, I will help you, I will uphold you with my victorious right hand' (RSV).

I was filled with anger when I read this. Why would I be dismayed? I couldn't understand why she had given me this. She knew what we had been through! I questioned why I needed to be strengthened, helped or upheld.

What was she thinking?

9

Shock Waves

Jasmine Esther Rutland was born in May 2002, weighing 5lbs 10oz. Labour had taken all day to kick start, but once it did, it was all done in fifteen minutes. The pain just took over; just one big, long contraction and Jasmine arrived! Delivering her that quickly was a bit of a shock. I had requested an epidural earlier in the day before labour had started, but in the end there was no time for that and this left me feeling quite cross. It was in this place of annoyance that I first saw Jasmine. The midwife had bundled her up in a blanket and was holding her beside me. I glanced at her face. I thought she looked weird, like some kind of being from outer space. She had two eyes, a nose and a mouth, but they were spaced out in a funny way. I angrily said, 'She looks like an alien,' and I turned my head away. I was still in recovery from her rapid arrival. The midwife took Jasmine to the baby resuscitation trolley to keep her warm until she was clothed. Relieved for the safe arrival of our third daughter, Andy cheerfully took out a nappy, a pink Babygro, a cardigan and a hat from our bag and between them, they got her dressed.

This time, as she was brought to me, I took her and I looked at her more closely and I agreed with my first impression, she seemed to have an odd look about her. I watched her as she opened and closed her eyes and moved her mouth around, and then I saw it. As Jasmine mouthed the air, she pushed her tongue out of her mouth.

'She looks as if she has Down's syndrome,' I said.

The midwife came to my side. 'Yes, she does have a different look about her.'

This was too much for Andy. In the space of a moment, relief turned to grief. He had reluctantly accepted the loss of Daniel and had seemed to stay strong following Zoe's health problems, but he couldn't deal with any more. He broke down in floods of tears; his heart was broken. I felt numb. The celebration of the arrival of new life had been stolen before. Now it had been stolen again, although this time in a different way. Our hopes and dreams for this new baby started to look very different from what we had imagined.

I was in a dazed state but I knew I needed to think practically and right now, my newborn baby was hungry. She latched onto my breast successfully and fed well. As I laid her back in the cot, a doctor came to tell us about the problems that babies with Down's syndrome can have.

'We will need to keep her in hospital so we can check her heart is working properly, and we will need to take some bloods from her to confirm what we think we are seeing.'

He asked me about the prenatal scans.

'Her statistic for having Down's syndrome was 1 in 3,500 when we had the twelve-week scan,' I said, 'and there was no concern about her heart formation at the twenty-week scan.'

He continued his explanation, 'People with Down's syndrome have a learning difficulty and they can have problems with eating and some can have problems with their bowels. They often have problems with speech and they can also be susceptible to leukaemia . . .' He went on about some physical differences Jasmine had, such as floppy limbs, creases on her palms, small ears and nasal passages.

I had heard enough. I was saturated with information about what was or could be. I cut him off in mid-flow.

'Stop,' I said. 'I can't take any more. Thank you for your time, but I need to rest now!'

He left the room and we took some deep breaths.

When we rang our parents with the bittersweet news, we were met with a sense of disbelief. I was not sure if this was because Jasmine had Down's syndrome or whether it was that life had thrown us another curveball. The girls were with my parents so this phone call was their cue to bring the girls in to see us.

Within an hour my parents and the girls had arrived, along with trepidation and curiosity. The room hung with uncertainty. Georgia was 2-and-a-half years old, Zoe was 5-and-a-half and both were ready to celebrate their new baby sister, unaware of the doubt that this little person was presenting to us adults. I was unsure of Georgia's take on the whole situation, but it wasn't long before Zoe was scanning the faces in the room to pick up clues for the undercurrent she felt.

Confused, she looked up into her daddy's face and asked, 'Why are you crying?' His tear-stained face crumpled again into quiet sobs.

My mum and dad looked helpless and I explained that Jasmine had something different about her and that we thought she had something called Down's syndrome. I spoke with a confidence about how we had a job to turn her 'downs into ups' and that everything would be OK. In reality, this was far from what I was really feeling. I had no clue about what lay ahead for us as a family, let alone for this little person who had just arrived.

Mum, Dad and the girls stayed for a while, and when they had gone, Andy's parents walked in. Andy could barely speak. His broken heart opened the floodgate of tears. We had a little time together before our room was needed and we were moved to the ward.

Jasmine needed to be monitored for various reasons. There was a room on the postnatal ward called the Transitional Care Unit. Jasmine and I were given a bed in there, but I wanted to leave. I didn't want to be in close proximity with other mums and I couldn't face conversation. I needed to retreat and contemplate my situation, and I didn't want Andy to leave. The rule of no dads staying over is fine in the normal run of events, but there was nothing normal about how life was unfolding for us.

As it turned out, we were very blessed; a private room had been arranged for us and it was set up with an extra foldout bed, so Andy could stay too. There was just about room for Jasmine's cot to squeeze in, and our room was next to the transitional care room where they had kept a bed space for her, in case we needed extra assistance. I was so grateful for the kindness we were being shown.

One of the things they wanted to monitor was Jasmine's heart. The prenatal scans hadn't shown any cardiac problems, so it was advisable for Jasmine to have a detailed cardiac exploration. We had to wait for a specialist to do this and they would monitor her until they were able to do the scan.

Her heart, her feeding and her floppy muscle tone were the medical focus for the time being. The transitional care midwife popped her head in frequently to see how we were doing.

Some hours had passed since Jasmine had been fed. I knew that Zoe and Georgia went for long periods of time between feeds in their first twenty-four hours, so I didn't think about disturbing Jasmine to feed her again too soon. By the early hours,

I was having trouble sleeping and I did think I ought to try to feed her. She was sleepy and groggy and she certainly wasn't interested in feeding. I thought I would check with the midwife and she decided to test Jasmine's blood sugars. They were quite low so she did need to have some milk. The midwife asked if I minded if Jasmine had a bottle, so they could see what, and if any, went in. I tried to push the teat into her mouth but she was having none of it!

I snapped. My practical, matter-of-fact approach was taken over by emotions. I couldn't do this. I called the midwife and asked her to take Jasmine away. I didn't think I had it within me to keep her and look after her, especially if she had a heart problem. The future seemed very uncertain. I was still carrying the stress of Zoe's health and even though her thyroxine levels were heading in the right direction, her sugar levels were still so erratic. I couldn't see how I was going to manage.

I lay in the small hours with my thoughts running in circles and the odd surge of adrenaline which made me feel slightly nauseous. The familiarity of grief revisited my mind. I was sleepless in this hospital room with Andy beside me and our baby in the room next door. It was like déjà vu, our hopes and dreams shattered into broken pieces, only this time the baby was alive. I was tormented by memories of losing Daniel along with facing fears of the future.

Andy was asleep. His breathing was soft and regular, but sleep evaded me. I couldn't stay in the room with my thoughts running wild. I got up and slipped quietly through the door, not quite sure of my destination. The corridors were dim and the stillness of the night was shaken by the distant sounds of newborn babies crying.

I found myself entering the transitional care room where Jasmine had been taken, and the midwife explained to me how she'd needed to spoon some milk into Jasmine's mouth. She had taken a few drops and her blood sugars had improved. Satisfied with this information, I walked away feeling very unsure about my new arrival. I turned down the corridor, away from Andy and Jasmine. I felt like walking away from my life. My legs moved me forward but my mind was somewhere else. I was drawn to a glow of light shining from the part-open door of the midwives' office. I popped my head round the door. Inside, I was met with a gentle and kind lady who welcomed me in and gave me her time. She gave me the space to ask a barrage of questions, most of which had no immediate answers, but I needed to ask them in order to process what was going on.

I asked her so many questions.

'What is the procedure if I choose to give my child up for adoption?'

'Can I get her back if I change my mind?'

'Where will she go?'

I knew I needed to keep my options open and this wasn't the time to be making firm decisions about anything. Everything was so muddled. I had no idea how I was going to cope or even if I could cope at all. The midwife was a good listener and seemed to know which of my questions were rhetorical and which ones I needed straight answers for. I came out of the room feeling a little clearer and at ease. I returned to the room where Andy was, climbed into bed and continued to muse over the situation. I cannot remember whether I was able to sleep, but as the new day emerged I'd come to a decision.

My decision was influenced by my midnight reflections along with the words on the bookmark Mum had given me the day before Jasmine was born. I don't think that my mum knew the significance of these words before Jasmine's arrival, but it brought hope into the situation and enabled me to move forward. I had made my decision and it was final.

'She is my baby and she is alive as I thought God had promised. I'm going to love her, nurture her and be her mum. I will do this with his help.'

Now I knew what that bookmark was all about! Those words were to be my encouragement and were another promise over me. They were given to me as a gift from God and in my misunderstanding, I had rejected them. My mum had intended to encourage me and I had received it as discouragement. I had been so wrong. Now that I could see more clearly, I was free to receive the blessing of my mother's encouragement and the blessing from God.

With this new resolve, I scooped Jasmine into my arms and accepted her as mine.

'Come on, Jas, let's do this,' I whispered to her.

A new chapter had begun.

Jasmine had her heart checked and to our relief, it was perfect and pumping with efficiency. Hurdle one had been jumped! We went home five days after her birth and all seemed well.

Feeding had started OK, but as my milk was in plentiful supply, Jasmine couldn't cope with the volume of liquid in her mouth. She would cough and splutter and her pattern of feeding would be interrupted by coughing on the milk. I tried feeding her in different positions and found that sometimes she coped and sometimes she didn't. I needed to lay muslin cloths round her neck to catch the milk that hadn't been swallowed but been expelled outwards. I had no idea how much she was taking in, but I knew the muslin was soaked at the end of feeding time. Feeding her would take such a long time, whether it was my breast or a bottle, that I was finding it hard to give Zoe and Georgia the attention that they needed. My stress levels began to rise. Sharing my time around was so imbalanced and alongside that, I had a growing concern that something was wrong with Jasmine.

When Jasmine was 2 weeks old I poured out my concerns to the health visitor. Jasmine was listless, pale and very sleepy. Breastfeeding was causing her to choke, and bottle feeding wasn't much better. Nothing seemed to prevent Jasmine from coughing and spluttering on her feeds. I also found it hard to be fair when managing Zoe's challenging behaviour and helping her to stay calm. I didn't know if it was to do with her sugar levels, her overactive thyroid, jealousy of her sister, or something else. I was grateful for my mum to be staying to support me and share this load, as Andy had gone back to work.

Added to this stress, my cat was hiding under the bed with what looked like a punctured eyeball. He must have had a fight in the night. I didn't know which way I should turn. I was weary and felt pushed from all sides. It was hard to prioritize. I cried, and then I cried some more.

The scene unravelled from here like a puppy pulling a toilet roll. Following the visit with the health visitor, I was instructed to take Jasmine to A & E as her breathing was laboured. My mum helped me get organized. I had managed to contact someone to help me deal with my cat and sadly, I had to part with him as I just didn't have the emotional resources to help him. Zoe and I took him to a house registered with Cats Protection. My emotions were screaming, 'This is all wrong! I should be able to deal with this!' I didn't want to lose him. The lady promised she'd look after him and produced papers for me to sign him over.

On the way home, Zoe said to me, 'Mummy, you do love me, don't you?'

'Of course, Zoe, I love you very much.'

She paused for a couple of seconds, 'Mummy, you won't give me away, will you?'

My heart lurched. I could understand her logic! I explained to her that she was our child and no matter how ill she was, we would never send her away. I told her she was loved so much more than our poorly cat, even though we had loved him too. I assured her I would never give her away to anyone.

When we arrived home, I swapped Zoe for Jasmine and headed to the local hospital. It was clear that Jasmine was very poorly. Her oxygen levels were low and the doctors needed to put needles and lines into her skin. This distress was all too much for me, so I walked away. I went outside the building, sat on a grass mound and sobbed. I called out, 'What is going on, God? I don't understand, haven't I had enough to handle so far? This feels like overload. I feel like a human punch-bag. Why? Why? Why?'

Jasmine was admitted to hospital. An X-ray confirmed that she had pneumonia which was stopping her from feeding correctly and preventing her from absorbing enough oxygen to breathe properly. I settled Jasmine onto the children's ward and rang my mum to ask her to bring in some clothes for her. In the face of the adrenalin surges, I wrestled with the fight or flight scenario. Everything within me screamed 'flight', to leave this scene because it was too hard to accept. I decided to leave Jasmine overnight, rather than stay with her. I was exhausted, battered and in addition to all of this, I felt guilty. What kind of mother leaves their newborn baby in hospital? I had no answers to this question. Zoe and Georgia needed me too. They noticed when I wasn't around. Jasmine wouldn't notice and I needed sleep in order to survive this turmoil. I repeated to myself over and over again, 'I won't feel guilty for leaving my 13-day-old baby in hospital.'

There wasn't a lot I could do for Jasmine, but I could supply her with breast milk. I went home via the shop to buy a breast pump and I would return in the morning with fresh supplies!

Jasmine's hospital visit lasted twelve days. Her requirement for oxygen prolonged her stay. These twelve days were very tough for me. I spent some nights at home and some in hospital. I tried to divide myself out between the girls. Georgia came and played in the hospital playroom on some days and she also started nursery for the first time. Zoe went to school and, in the middle of it all, my mum returned home. It felt like the balls I had been juggling were falling all around me.

Andy had taken his paternity leave in the first week of Jasmine's life and had been busy working while Mum was around. Now, I needed him to help me as well as work! We were very blessed to have some good friends who were willing to look after Zoe and Georgia while I was looking after Jasmine in hospital so Andy could continue to work as much as possible.

We were in unknown territory. Our lives, once again, had been turned upside down and we had no idea where this road was leading. It was at this time someone told me about a poem they had read called 'Welcome to Holland' by Emily Perl Kingsley. It was about going on a journey to Italy and preparing to visit the different places there but when you arrived, you realized you weren't in Italy, you were in Holland. Obviously, this would be a bit of a shock as this wasn't what you expected. However, as you were there, you might as well have a look around and when you do, you find that you enjoy Holland a great deal, even if it isn't Italy.

I could certainly relate to this.

We weren't expecting life to be like this. We knew we were having another daughter and we were full of expectations that her life would be healthy and blessed. We thought that her childhood would lead to adulthood and she would be able to live an independent life. We needed to be prepared to take on a different viewpoint and accept that we had arrived in 'Holland' even though we had prepared for 'Italy'.

10

What on Earth?

One time when we were in hospital, someone told me of a poem that had helped them when they had been in a similar situation. This poem by Erma Bombeck was called 'A Special Mother'. It was about God choosing which mother would have a child with a disability and how he would help her to look after them. It spoke of being happy and giving the child joy. It talked about the patience, independence and selfishness of that mother and how she had to balance these things, so she would be able to give to the child and still sustain herself. It also spoke of appreciating the simple achievements that would normally go unnoticed but said that this mother would see miracles and rejoice in those small achievements. The thing that caught my attention was the word 'selfishness'. I was the mum who said, 'No, you can't share my chocolate bar, it's mine!' I was the mum who put the children to bed early so I could have an evening to myself, knowing that I would be a better mum for the next day. I was selfish and felt relieved that this seemingly negative trait was something I could turn around and use in a positive way! The poem said that God would be by my side, which I found so moving, as these words echoed those of the verse that my mum had given me on the bookmark. I was not to fear because God would give me the strength to get through and he promised to stand by my side at all times.

I found comfort in these words as I flitted to and from the hospital, wanting to be with Zoe and Georgia as well as with Jasmine, and needing to stay at home sometimes where I could get proper sleep to cope with it all. I decided it was OK to leave Jasmine on her own some nights. I was so encouraged by this poem, it was very timely and very helpful to me.

Due to my experiences, I have changed my expectations about all sorts of things over the years. I've come to realize that expecting too much has led me to disappointment. On the other hand, having lower expectations and a heart of gratitude seems to reveal all number of little gifts. I've come to see that most people strive to do their best and, for all sorts of reasons, expectations aren't always met. I have learnt to be accommodating when things don't go my way and I delight when things succeed and go well. I've also found that when things have gone wrong, there has always been a solution or a compromise and I have learnt something valuable about life along the way.

While pregnant with Jasmine, I had expectations which were not met in the reality of her birth. I was disappointed and, at the time, I saw her as a misfit. She wasn't going to fulfil the same dreams I had for her before I knew she had Down's syndrome. After a process of time and contemplation, I realized that I could still dream for this little person – she still had value, purpose and a future. It was just going to be different to how I imagined. There was no point in worrying and anticipating the future or what the dream – or nightmare – might look like. I had a vulnerable and poorly baby to care for today, and if I wanted her home and well, then caring today was what mattered.

When Jasmine was finally well enough to come home, we had a little party. We blew up balloons, played pass the parcel with the girls and enjoyed some party food. It was an extra celebration that we hadn't expected. Family life resumed once more and the pressure of living in two places was eliminated.

Episodes of trauma can be like climbing a mountain. The terrain is rough, walking feels heavy and it takes effort to keep going. Energy is sucked out of you quicker than you can refuel. The direction of the mountain path is sometimes obvious and while it's steep and tiring, at least you can see your way ahead. But mountains can have corners and turns which bring unexpected stumbling blocks. The unknown around the corner brings its own fears and challenges. We had reached the mountaintop once more, where the view of the past and present was more visible. It was an interesting point to pause and reflect and to dream again.

The majority of babies with Down's syndrome are slower to grasp the milestones. Jasmine was about nine weeks old when she smiled for the first time. What a joyous occasion it was. It was like a little miracle had occurred and we were delighted!

Feeding her continued to be a huge challenge. It would take so long and she'd often gag and choke. I found breastfeeding her a trial. The flow of milk was like a jet hose into Jasmine's mouth and I'd end up wearing most of the milk! I would often express milk and put it in a bottle and this eventually became the way of feeding following another hospital admission. This still didn't solve the coughing completely. I tried all sorts of shapes and sizes of different teats to see if I could stem the flow of fluid, but nothing seemed to improve the spluttering during feeding.

When Jasmine reached 4 months, her breathing became laboured once more. Another hospital admission was needed and I was asked questions about her feeding. Jasmine had pneumonia again and needed extra oxygen as her lungs were struggling to provide enough. Again, she was wired to drips and had antibiotics pumped in to fight the infection. My poor baby. I felt so helpless.

Another three weeks of ferrying back and forth followed. Zoe still needed lots of support dealing with her injections, administering her insulin, planning her food and taking her to school. Georgia needed dropping off and picking up from nursery on her allotted days. Andy needed to keep working and I needed to juggle it all and keep going!

It was this admission that exposed the root issue of Jasmine's feeding difficulties. She was aspirating on her milk. In other words, the milk was not only going down the pipe to the stomach, as it should, but it was also going into her lungs. She was diagnosed with a neurological delay of messages travelling from her brain to her swallow reflex and we were told this was a permanent defect that would affect her ability to feed for the rest of her life. The solution was to bypass feeding in the normal way, so once she'd got over her infection, Jasmine came home with a nasogastric tube. She was no longer allowed to feed orally. All her milk was to go into the tube, which was stuck onto her cheek and then passed up her nostril and straight down to the stomach.

My background in nursing was the provision we needed and while I wished we could see Jasmine's face without the tube, I was grateful for the confidence I had in handling the practicalities of tube feeding. It certainly eased the pressures of time constraints of bottle feeding as this only took around ten to fifteen minutes and it allowed me some more time to give to Zoe and Georgia.

Zoe, in particular, had struggled with all the coming and going and was quite angry with the people around her. Juggling her diabetes with food intake was a challenge and we experienced a number of stressful mealtimes.

Motherhood wasn't quite how I'd imagined!

Through the trials, motherhood showed me something of the intensity of love. 'Love is patient and kind. Love is not jealous, it does not brag, and is not proud. Love is not rude, it is not selfish, and it cannot be made angry easily. Love does not remember wrongs done against it. Love is never happy when others do wrong, but it is always happy with the truth. Love never gives up on people. It never stops trusting, never loses hope, and never quits' (1 Cor. 13:4–7, ERV). I realized I had a lot of work to do to love like this, but it gave me a framework to practise my love in motherhood. I believe it was the essence of God's love that enabled me to survive the demands of my young and needy family.

Following the nasogastric tube insertion, we were blessed with a couple of months of easier routine.

It was during this time, one morning, I received a phone call from the hospital playroom manager saying they would like to offer us a family break away to somewhere of our choice! I was overwhelmed. A real break away for me, meant leaving Jasmine behind. I found this difficult but felt it was justified as I reflected on the words in the poem I had been given. I asked my mum and dad to have Jasmine for a week so Andy, Zoe, Georgia and I could to fly off to Tenerife in the October half-term. We had a wonderful time away to refuel.

By the end of November, when Jasmine was 6 months old, I noticed a new issue. She would twitch her arms, legs and head inwards and follow that with a small cry. It happened intermittently and regularly throughout the day. I raised this during a phone call to the paediatrician and he decided it would be best to admit Jasmine so they could observe her.

We were put into a single room at the end of the ward. It was reasonably spacious and had a large window for natural light. It was well set-up with a bed and a cot for us both, but I couldn't believe we were here again. The familiarity somehow eased my tension and we settled in quickly as I knew the routine. The staff welcomed us as if we'd arrived home!

I was almost sure they were going to tell me that Jasmine had epilepsy, so I wasn't surprised when various brain activity scans were on the timetable for the next day. We spent the next five days looking at the diagnosis and treatment of a condition called West syndrome, which is also known as infantile spasms (a type of epilepsy) and the paediatricians conferred with one another to seek out the right medication to deal with it.

By the time the weekend arrived, I was exhausted. I needed some time alone to retreat and refuel. I felt so low. With Jasmine being looked after in hospital and Andy looking after Zoe and Georgia for the weekend, I packed a bag and drove to my mum and dad's house. Here I found the solace and time to sleep that I so desperately needed. I even took some time to write down some of my thoughts.

I was emotionally drained; I didn't think I could take any more. It was like my cupboard was full, its doors bulging and there was no room for anything else. I couldn't believe that Jasmine now had epilepsy as well. I sat there holding on to four years of pain, and I wept.

I realized that I had forgotten to eat a few days previously. I couldn't see how I was going to carry on if I had lost focus on even caring for myself. I felt disconnected. I wondered if this detachment was my coping mechanism. I had been told that I was admired for how well I coped, but I didn't think I wanted to be detached. Or maybe I did. Perhaps I needed to be detached. The recent events made me feel like I had been walking in a desert for days and days, looking for water and not being able to find it. I was exhausted. I wanted things to be easier. I didn't want to feel loss any more. I didn't want the difficulties of life to be dictated to me any more. I wanted to be in control and make it all better.

I felt like my life had been stolen. Somebody came four years before and hijacked my life. They took my son away and they presented me with fear again. They interrupted childhood for Zoe, giving her diabetes and thyroid problems. They gave me a child I never asked for and then made me suffer as I tried to make the best of a situation that seemed to be going from bad to worse.

After I had raged about my situation, I found myself asking how to lift myself from this place of misery. I didn't want to stay here. I couldn't change the situation, but I had options in how I chose to respond. I had been here before, asking the same questions, and I knew my goal was to experience some peace, contentment and joy in each day. While I thought that was unlikely to be achievable every day, my mind was set in that direction and I was going to learn how to do it!

My reflection time was interrupted as the phone rang in the distance. It was Andy ringing me to say that the doctors were concerned about Jasmine's breathing being rapid. My adrenalin kicked in once again and I knew I had to return to face life at home. I felt like I was being battered, torn and attacked. I couldn't do anything to fight it. Life just had to roll on, but I felt broken and destroyed.

11

Traumatized

I don't remember how I got back that day, but I found Jasmine in a sorry state when I arrived. Her colour was pale, her body was limp and she was lying there struggling in her quest for oxygen. A doctor was leaning over her bedside, trying to work out how he could get intravenous access given that Jasmine's veins were hidden from view. The only option he had was to use a vein in her scalp. I watched with sadness as he shaved off a patch of her downy hair so he could fix the cannula in place. Her breathing was so fast and her oxygen levels were dipping in and out of the normal range.

The doctors thought that pneumonia had set in again and were pumping in antibiotics to try to settle Jasmine's breathing. They had hoped they would have seen signs of improvement by now, but instead she was getting worse. Her oxygen requirements were reaching limits that they could not reach. She was too poorly to feed and was only receiving intravenous fluids. She would make the odd whimper, but she was too ill to even cry and her heart rate was more than 200 beats a minute. All the while this was going on, I received a phone call from Zoe's school saying that I needed to collect her, as she had cut her head open on a desk at school and it needed steristripping (Steri-Strips are sticky paper strips which cover and hold a small wound together). I felt numb.

The following day the local paediatric team had exhausted all their resources to support Jasmine's breathing requirements and she now needed to be ventilated, which meant moving her to a specialist hospital.

I have never experienced adrenalin quite like I did in that 24-hour period. The icy cold surges would rush down my arms and legs. My insides felt like they were being pulled downwards and my heart thumped loudly inside my chest as if it was trying to jump out. Cold sweat covered my entire body and I felt sick, knowing that Jasmine was on the cusp of life and death. All I could do was pray for life to win.

Our minister came to visit us while arrangements were being made to move Jasmine to intensive care in London, and he kindly brought me a bag of overnight items that I would need while away. I was interested to see that the carrier bag he had chosen had a large rainbow on it. I hoped this would be significant.

Jasmine was retrieved by the emergency ambulance team. Andy and I released her to the team and agreed to meet them there. We were wretched. Over the last few hours, we had overheard the medics responding to Jasmine's fight with life and death. Our bodies felt like they had been physically attacked by adrenalin. We needed to take some deep breaths before we got into the car and made our way in pursuit.

As we entered intensive care, I noticed there was a calmness there that I hadn't expected. Jasmine was on the left of the room lying unconscious in a cot, which was surrounded by monitors on either side. She had tubing snaking around her body. One was going into her mouth, others went into her arms and legs. The cannula that had been put in her scalp had one coming out from it too. It was like she had become trapped in the coils of a snake. Would the snake loosen its grip and slither away, or would it take my daughter as its prey?

Despite all of this, she looked peaceful and unaware of the jungle of doubt and fear that surrounded her. There was very little we could do and, as it was about 4 a.m., we were shown to a room next door where one of us could rest. We decided Andy would go home to be with the girls when they woke.

The next morning, I awoke a little disorientated. I could hear the air-conditioning and distant beeping sounds, and I became aware of a heaviness within me. I took some deep breaths before I stood up to go to see Jasmine.

I walked through the doors and made my way to the left and I was relieved to find that the scene I had left the night before looked pretty much the same. A new nurse was in charge of Jasmine and she met me with a confident smile. I greeted her.

'I'm Jasmine's mum. How is she?'

'We think Jasmine has caught two types of respiratory virus. She is very ill and we are doing everything we can for her,' she said.

'Is she going to be OK?' I asked.

There was a pause before she responded, which made me feel sick. Her eyes told me what she was thinking before her lips uttered, 'We don't know, children with these viruses quite often get worse before they get better, we just have to wait.'

So here I was, face-to-face with the fragility of life again. I had no control over the outcome. I just had to wait.

I felt like I was back in the desert, only instead of walking I was standing still, stunned, burning and scorched by the heat. I had nowhere to hide – there was no covering from the exposure of pain.

A day passed and nothing changed. I was suspended in a dark void as I went to the room next door to sleep that night. I held a picture of Jasmine in my mind and wondered if the rainbow carrier bag was a sign of hope and prayed that I would return in the morning to an improvement.

It was early the next morning when I awoke and went to see Jasmine. Sleep had not helped me; I felt heavy and my head ached. As I approached her bedside, I could see extra equipment around her cot. The nurse looking after her must have been observing my reactions, as the first thing she did was to tell me about the new machine they had rigged up for her. It was called an oscillator, a different type of ventilating machine to the other one she had. I could hear a drilling noise coming from it and I noticed that her chest was no longer rising and falling. Her face and limbs seemed puffy and her chest shook with vibrations from the oscillator. I wasn't sure that I recognized her as my Jasmine, but the name on the charts indicated that this indeed was my girl.

'Jasmine has had a difficult night,' the nurse said. 'Her oxygen levels dropped to unsafe levels and we were unable to improve them, so we brought in this new machine as it changes how the oxygen can enter. We also had to give her nitric gas as it can help with this type of ventilation.'

All I could do was listen and nod my head.

The nurse continued, 'She is very sick and we can't pretend that she is through the worst yet.'

I could hear my heart beating in my ears and I thought I might throw up; I could feel tears forming and knew I had to get out of there. As I turned to leave, the nurse spoke gently again, 'Time will see this through; we are looking after her; we just need to wait.'

I thanked her with a trembling voice and left the room.

I couldn't stay. I needed to shut my emotions down, lock them away for another time, so I wasn't able to feel the pain. I rang Andy to come and take over, I was too scared to see her being resuscitated and not making it. I was sure I wouldn't ever get over the memory of that and what I didn't see, I wouldn't remember. Andy came and took my place of vigil at her bed-side. I thanked him for releasing me and I walked away from the hospital with my head down. This hurt, no matter how much I tried to deny the pain. It was evening as I left and began my journey home. I looked around at the gloomy streets and saw rows of closed, lifeless shops and I wondered where God was in all this. My world was colourless and dark. The rainbow of promise I yearned for was nowhere in sight. The word 'trau-matized' barely even scratched the surface of how I felt.

Zoe and Georgia were being looked after by my friend Julie and I wanted to be with them. It was late as I drew up on the drive of Julie's house. Zoe and Georgia were in their beds when I got back so I snuck in, kissed their cheeks and wished them a silent goodnight. I would have to wait until morning to scoop them into my arms and pretend that my world wasn't all out at sea.

The girls kept me going in the storm of worry over the next few days. They returned home and although I was probably a little absent to them in some ways, at least they could see me and I could take Zoe to school and play with Georgia and pretend it was like any other ordinary day. I kept in constant contact with intensive care to get the latest update on Jasmine's progress. For ten days, there was no news of improvement, but at least there was no bad news either.

Finally, I got the news I had been praying for. Andy rang me to say she was through the worst and was managing to breathe with less support. All of a sudden, I felt so emotional, relief washed over me and I felt like a heavy weight had shifted off me. I felt safe to return to be with her now she was recovering. I was grateful to the dedicated staff who helped Jasmine fight her battle. It was a battle she would have lost if it weren't for them and their expertise.

Andy greeted me at the hospital door when I arrived. He looked tired and had grown a beard. Jasmine was still in the same position as she had been when I had left. It was like life had been on pause; however, I knew many people had been praying during this time, so I knew much activity had been going on in the background. Jasmine was still unconscious and as I leaned over the cot bars and medical equipment to kiss her cheek, I knew my baby was going to make it.

Andy and I briefly conversed about what Zoe and Georgia were doing, before he headed home to take over there. After he'd gone, I sat down beside Jasmine's cot. I reached through the bars and held her chubby little hand. I was yearning to gather her in my arms and hold her, but I knew I would have to wait for another time.

As I sat there, I started to allow my emotions some space in my life again and I became aware of my guilt. I asked myself, 'What kind of mother walks away from a child who was critically ill?' Was there a flaw in my character? Had I failed? I felt ashamed, but a small voice in the back of my mind was telling me it was necessary for survival and a little selfishness was OK.

I started to justify my actions for leaving Jasmine. There was nothing I could have offered her to influence the outcome. She hadn't needed me, she was unconscious, I didn't want to watch her die, I couldn't cope with seeing her like this. My list helped me battle away the guilt and I decided I'd made the right choice, that for me, leaving Jasmine in the care of the hospital and her daddy was OK and I had no need to carry guilt with me.

The next day she regained consciousness and I was at last able to have a cuddle with her. She was weak and had lost much of her muscle control, but she was alive. Still attached to her wires, she smiled up at me and I cried tears of joy and relief. The rainbow on the bag had been a sign. God had been faithful.

It was a slow recovery. Jasmine continued to require breathing support from the hospital for a couple more weeks and she had another serious little blip which gave great cause for concern, but she fought back and survived that too. Over the months that followed, she needed to regain strength and relearn skills. She'd lost the ability to sit independently so we knew she'd need to relearn balance. This, in part, could have been to do with her infantile spasms which were now under control with medication, but we also wondered whether her brain had been damaged from the times she had insufficient oxygen. Time would tell.

We arrived back home two days before Christmas and we celebrated in style. We were so grateful to God for restoring our daughter and saving her life. It felt like we had received a heavenly gift. People all around us had been praying for her and I believed these prayers were answered. My faith increased as I had seen and experienced the hand of God and he had shown his power and authority. This helped me to believe in something beyond the here and now.

I was thankful that we had survived the last month and this gratitude seemed to compensate for the trauma, even if it didn't cancel it all out. I began to appreciate the simple things after this. I took Jasmine into the shopping centre just after Christmas and she was mesmerized by the Christmas lights. I felt such a joy at the simplicity of being able to watch her in these ordinary moments.

I journaled a great deal during this time and this helped me to get perspective on the things that mattered. I also found that this was therapeutic in getting my emotions out and helped me to reflect. The year 2002 had been eventful and our lives had collided with all sorts of people we would never have met under different circumstances. It opened my eyes to see the importance and value of relationships.

Another positive thing to come out of it all was the fact that we had met some lovely social workers who could see life was tough for us, both at hospital and at home. The care we received was provided by a local charity who specialized in care for children with special needs. It so happened that my friend Julie worked for this organization and was able to be our assigned carer. I was immediately at ease knowing that Jasmine was in the hands of someone capable of caring for her with her feeding tube and who loved her like her own! Julie would take care of Jasmine once a week and I was able to have a break and spend some quality time with Zoe and Georgia. This care extended over the years with additional hours, and Jasmine would go for tea at Julie's home regularly too. In fact by the time Jasmine reached her teenage years, Julie's daughters Christina and Amy would take on this role and they became great friends. Life would have been very different without this special family on board.

We also qualified for help from an organization called Home-Start who specialize in providing support for families with pre-school children who, for whatever reason, find life a challenge. We met a wonderful volunteer who would come over once a week and look after the girls, in particular Georgia, who needed some fun times playing when I just needed to sleep.

We were so blessed with a fantastic social worker who, until she retired, journeyed alongside us through many difficult times. She was a brilliant advocate. She supported me and encouraged me to be the best mum I could be. I was aware that many other families didn't have great support, so all I could do was to appreciate her and be grateful.

Again and again I was reminded of the promise on the bookmark about God giving me strength and help. I felt overwhelmed with relief.

The year 2003 started well; I was able to find a routine that meant I could enjoy motherhood more. Each of the girls were developing their own little personalities and I wanted to take in as much as I could from them. Zoe made me laugh with her frank observations on life, and Georgia would want to be close beside me as we looked at books together. Jasmine found her voice and would lay on the floor cooing and chuckling when the girls lay with her. Andy helped out when he could, but in the main, was relieved to be able to work without the pressures of his family being split between home and hospital. However, this was not to last.

Jasmine got sick again with her breathing and was admitted to hospital once more for eight days which was followed by a week at home and then an admission to Great Ormond Street Hospital for her to have a permanent feeding tube.

I was expecting this visit as we had been on a waiting list. Five months beforehand, a decision had been made following various investigations on Jasmine's swallow, that the tube fixed to her face which passed down her nose and into her stomach was a temporary solution to being nil by mouth. Quite apart from the fact we missed seeing her lovely face free of tape and tube and now nine months old, Jasmine had become adept at finding a space to hook her finger into and whip the whole tube out! It wasn't straightforward to push back down, so the answer to this was to make a hole through the stomach wall and insert a small T-bar into it, which you could attach feeding tubes to. This would give access straight into the stomach for feeding. It was called a gastrostomy.

As Jasmine was in theatre, the sun shone into the empty hospital room I was in. I was recovering from that helpless, sinking feeling that parents experience when their child is being anaesthetized. Jasmine had struggled against the mask, her eyes had rolled back as the gas took effect and her arms flopped down once she had fallen asleep. I had experienced this with Zoe when she had her tonsils out. The surgeons told me that they were going to wrap the top of Jasmine's stomach around the bottom of her oesophagus, which would help to stop the reflux she had. I hoped this would stop her continual chest infections. A nurse popped her head through the door to check I was OK and reassured me they would call me when Jasmine woke up.

12

Recovery

The surgery was successful but it took Jasmine a long time to recover. We should have been in and out in three days, but for some reason her stomach went into shock and stopped working. In the three weeks we spent there, we endured a number of unplanned procedures to investigate what had gone wrong, all the while battling with Jasmine's need of nutrition. She underwent three anaesthetics in total instead of the one that was planned.

During this stay, my emotions followed a path much like that of a rollercoaster groaning up the track and plummeting down in the valley, with added speed to fuel my adrenalin. This time I'd lost contact with hope and I was swallowed up by self-pity. I was scared to ask God to make Jasmine better just in case my prayer went unheard or I didn't like the answer. I didn't want to be disappointed or confused if God didn't answer how I thought he should, so I avoided praying. I was anxious and agitated and I needed strength and peace instead. I was fed up and just wanted life to be normal.

I couldn't do this alone. The gift of being part of a church meant that I didn't have to. I received some timely visitors who were like angels to me. They prayed the prayers I couldn't. I felt awkward with them, but I was equally touched that they'd made the effort to come up to London to see us. I would see if there was any point of praying in the course of time.

While we were at the hospital, I met some very brave people who had courageous stories to tell. Their needs seemed far greater than mine. It was good to share stories. It helped me with feelings of isolation and I felt encouraged to support each of them. Being part of their lives helped me to change my perspective and caused me to stop thinking about myself so much. I realized that my own story wasn't that bad and that there were far worse things that could be happening to me. I was reminded to have a spirit of gratefulness and I am sure this attitude helped me to cope.

After the visit from my church friends, we didn't wait long for Jasmine's stomach to start working again and we were homeward bound at last.

Within ten days of returning home, we were packing our bags for hospital once again. This time it was for Georgia to have her tonsils taken out and grommets inserted due to continual chest infections and hearing loss, which were all to improve once this was done. The blessing of this was that Georgia and I had some quality time together, uninterrupted by the need of either of her siblings. We did jigsaws together, read books and cuddled up. In fact, Georgia had barely opened her eyes from the anaesthetic before she was staggering across the corridor, eager for the next interaction with her mum. She was going to squeeze the most she could out of it! She recovered well with nothing to report on and we hoped life would settle down with an easier pattern. We really wanted to spend more time at home than in hospital.

Unfortunately, the pattern for the next year that followed was more of the same. Jasmine's health continued to cause concern and we learnt how to adapt to the to-ing and fro-ing that each admission brought with it. We learnt how to rely on friends to support us with looking after Zoe and Georgia. We were very grateful for them. Jasmine's chest infections were a regular occurrence and she battled with low oxygen levels when she fell asleep.

She was nil by mouth and we knew she wasn't refluxing into her lungs following the surgery at Great Ormond Street, so we couldn't work out why she continued to have these episodes.

Hospital became primarily a place where Jasmine could be hooked up to an oxygen supply until the infection had passed. It was during one of these stays that one of the doctors noted her very large tonsils and posed the question about her having them removed. This was by no means straightforward, given her medical history of chest infections. The question was tossed about by the various professionals looking after her. They decided to investigate her breathing function to see if there was a reason why she was having so many chest infections and low oxygen levels and booked her in for a bronchoscopy which revealed that she had left bronchial stenosis. This meant that air entry into her left lung was compromised because her left bronchus (the tube entering the lung) was a squashed, flat shape rather than open and round. In addition, Jasmine was also struggling to manage her saliva. That wasn't a problem on its own, but she kept inhaling it and it would sit in the entrance of her lungs. I was relieved that they had established why she struggled to keep her oxygen levels up, but then I was frustrated that they reported that there was nothing they could do about the situation. They also decided that a tonsillectomy wouldn't help, but at least we knew why Jasmine needed oxygen so regularly. For some reason the paediatrician wasn't keen on setting up oxygen at home, so hospital became a regular event for a while. It was unsatisfactory, but there was little I could do, other than pray it would get better. I had to get on with it.

The relationships between the doctors, nurses and myself took on a familiarity, which made the whole situation more bearable. Each time we arrived on the ward it was like we'd come to our second home. It was amazing how I adapted, and while there were moments I just wanted it to end, I found I had some kind of strength to keep going.

Filling time while in hospital was never a problem, as I found myself connecting with the other families. We would listen, support and share our significant life events. I took on a maternal role to new families coming in, welcoming them and showing them the ropes as well as acknowledging the stress of dealing with their sick child. It was an eye-opening experience and I became acutely aware of the uniqueness of our lives. Some people on the ward seemed to be worse off, which again made me grateful that my situation wasn't as bad. Equally, some people were challenged by something that I would view as simple. I learnt that everybody had their own story, and however they experienced it, they had their own way of dealing with it.

It was a gruelling year, but I gained some valuable insights into life. One of the things I learnt to do was to compartmentalize. I had a hospital life, a home life and a church life.

Although I craved a normal family life, I realized that moments with Andy and the girls were to be cherished and not to be taken for granted, so I learnt to treasure our time together, which somehow made it more precious.

I found it difficult to relax, as I was not quite sure when the next hospital admission would happen. I poured my all into trying to be the best mum I could be and at times, I know, I neglected Andy. He was very supportive during split family periods when Jasmine was in hospital, and did the best job he could as Dad in loving and caring for his daughters. There were times where we just had to put 'us' on hold, simply in order to survive the intensity of looking after our girls. Our love must have had solid foundations; there were times when the pressure was so great, it made us question what being married was all about, but we didn't give up. Hope remained and enabled us to endure all sorts of circumstances.

Our support came from friends, church family, social workers and psychologists. The wonderful medical professionals carried out their duties and, although we didn't always agree on a code of practice, we all had Jasmine's best interests at heart.

We continued to feed Jasmine via her gastrostomy, but I was keen to revisit this diagnosis to see if anything had changed. With the guidance of a speech and language therapist, we trialled Jasmine on and off with pureed foods. However, her frequent chest infections disrupted the process, and because it was unknown whether feeding her was partly causing the trouble, we were advised to stop giving anything by mouth again. This position brought turmoil to my mind. I either refused to see or I just couldn't imagine a life with no food. I found such pleasure in food, along with the social interaction that often takes place at mealtimes. Jasmine would miss out on so much of life's pleasures without it. I didn't like this, but given the circumstances of her health, I followed their advice.

After a number of other hospital admissions, the subject of tonsils came up again and it was finally decided that Jasmine would benefit from a tonsillectomy due to her repeating pattern of infections. This procedure would create more breathing space once the cumbersome glands were out of the way. I was on the verge of desperation in terms of caring for Jasmine's medical needs. I became convinced that once her tonsils came out, she'd not only stop getting so many chest infections but that she would also be able to eat again. In one consultation, I became very animated and shared my hope for her to eat after her surgery, but I was quickly reprimanded and told I was being unrealistic. I was told the reason for her 'nil by mouth' status was because of her neurological responses, not enlarged tonsils. Jasmine had her swallow reflex rechecked to see if there had been any improvement in the neurological delay since the last test. This appointment was to bring a very significant moment in our journey.

I did not accept that Jasmine would need to have a gastrostomy forever. It was awful for her as it leaked stomach acid around the outside of the stoma (hole), causing the skin on her tummy to be raw and painful. She'd wriggle around in bed and get tangled in the tubing; on numerous occasions it became unattached and the milk would go all over the bed instead of into her. I also had to make sure she couldn't get her hands inside her clothing or she'd pull the device straight out.

Apart from the practicalities of having a gastrostomy, I wanted Jasmine to be able to sit at the table and enjoy a meal with her family and to have her taste buds triggered by flavours from regular meals. I wanted her to use the muscles in her mouth to prepare her for talking. My dreams and desires for her seemed to be so unachievable. I was desperate for the circumstances to change for her. I found myself pleading with God again, asking him to change things and to fix the problem. He'd saved her before, so there was always hope.

In the car, on our way to the swallow test, I was anxious and I prayed, 'Please God, make this gastrostomy temporary.' As I was calling out, a powerful sense of peace came over me; it was like I had received a silent 'yes', and the tears of relief began to fall.

I went into the test room full of hope that they would tell me everything was OK, but this was not to be. The test showed that Jasmine's swallow was worse than they had thought, so we must carry on as we were. I was gutted. With my head low, I made my way back to the car with Jasmine. I sat in the car and fired my frustrated questions to God.

What was this hope and peace all about?

Had I misinterpreted it?

Why had I felt so sure it would all work out, only two hours before?

As I sat there with a downcast heart, I looked up and there, through the windscreen, bold and vibrant, was a rainbow. I couldn't believe it.

This moment was the beginning of another new promise. It was a moment where my hope went deeper and I began to believe with certainty that Jasmine's gastrostomy was temporary; that despite what any test told us about the state of her abilities, God knew otherwise and that in time, the issue would be fixed.

Jasmine had her tonsils taken out in June 2004 at the age of 2. It was a particularly tricky case due to her 'nil by mouth' status and her fluctuating oxygen levels. The hospital had prepared well and had ensured that an intensive care bed would be available post-op in the event of breathing difficulties. It was successful, with one precautionary night spent in intensive care and, as she was well enough, she went to an ordinary ward after that. It was usual to stay one night in hospital following a tonsillectomy, but we were told that we would need to stay in hospital for three weeks because Jasmine was nil by mouth. Swallowing food was one of the most important aspects of recovery, so she had a high risk of post-op infection, which would have caused bleeding. Fortunately, none of this happened and we were able to go home after two weeks.

I had pinned my hopes on Jasmine's tonsillectomy being an end to all the problems regarding breathing and eating. I know

I'd been told having her tonsils out wouldn't make any difference to her ability to eat, but I still wasn't convinced! I had not been able to let go of this thought, and it was with this hope that one day I took a course of action which could have been disastrous.

The day after we came home from hospital, I woke with determination to help Jasmine recover as best and as quickly as possible from her surgery. We'd had an uneventful two-week period in hospital, which was good, but if the best way to recover was to eat, now that I was at home, who was there to stop me giving Jasmine food?

It started with a thought that I should give Jasmine some toast. I played with the idea for a while. I was aware of the potential hazards, but for some reason, I was drawn to take the risk. The thought grew and grew until it took hold and fixed itself in my mind. Spurred on by the 'rainbow moment' after the swallow test, I put some bread in the toaster. I placed the telephone on the table beside me, in case I needed to ring for an ambulance. I put Jasmine in her high chair but left the straps off, in case I needed to get her out quickly. Energized by adrenalin, I put some butter on the toast and broke off a small piece. Before any sense of doubt could stop me, I popped it into Jasmine's mouth. I sat there nervously, ready to grab her to save her from choking. My eyes fixated on her mouth, watching to see what would happen next.

13

Miracles Do Happen!

What I saw that day is something I will never forget. Jasmine, the proud owner of only four front teeth, began to chew and move the toast around her mouth before successfully swallowing it and looking for more!

Jasmine had no progressive practise in eating, she was deemed medically unsafe and yet miraculously had the ability to eat like she'd always been doing it. Over the following weeks, pieces of toast progressed to chopped meals and Jasmine never looked back.

Her health improved, she came off her epilepsy medication, she no longer had chest infections or inhaled her saliva, and we were able to concentrate on helping her reach her milestones and simply enjoy her being our child. Hospital admissions became a thing of the past and we were able to experience family time together for the first time in years. I was so ready for this. The continual upheavals had begun to take their toll and I was exhausted by our pattern of life. I had been feeling like a hamster on a wheel, running and running but going nowhere for two years.

My unorthodox behaviour obviously caused some concern with Jasmine's paediatrician, and unfortunately the speech and language therapist couldn't condone my actions and our working relationship ended there.

The gastrostomy needed to stay in place because Jasmine still couldn't manage to swallow liquids without coughing and spluttering, as the speed at which fluid moved was still faster than her swallow reflex. I was satisfied that having Jasmine sitting at the table with us, eating a normal meal, was an answer to my prayers.

The elation of this outcome filled my spirit with a deep and indescribable contentment. My appreciation for what for many is a 'normal' thing taught me to search deeper into my expectations and not to take any aspect of my life for granted. Maybe one day I would be able to see the fulfilment of the promise (eating was half the battle; fluids were the second half!), but for now, I would rest.

I went through a period of time where I marvelled at how wonderful life was for us. God had carried us in the dark times and brought us through the storm into calmer waters. Life was precious and daily routine was cherished. Finally, we were on an even keel. We could enjoy our family in our own home and had time to invest back into our friendships, now we were over the 'hump' of illnesses. I had been traumatized by the events of the past two years and it was time to reflect and do some healing.

Thankful that we were in a much steadier place, I began to feel more 'normal'. I had grieved many things; Daniel's death, how diabetes had robbed Zoe of a part of her childhood, Jasmine having Down's syndrome and all that brought with it. I had grieved what I perceived to be a normal family life. But now, as I stopped to reflect, I was able to see my situation from various angles and I could see a bigger picture. From one view, something may have seemed pointless, painful and wrong, but from another angle I could see purpose, healing and maybe even some good.

That year, two of my friends experienced tragedy. Within a month of each other, they both lost their daughters – aged 2 and 3. Their trauma made me see the many good things I had in my life. I was devastated for my friends and I wished I could bring back their girls, or at least try to protect them from their pain. I felt helpless, but somehow I knew that I could be a supportive friend to them in their dark places. I understood grief, even if I didn't know how it felt to be in their shoes. I was able to join them on their journey for a season. I was honoured to be included in their lives at such a vulnerable time, and I prayed that I was helping them to get to a more manageable place; that my story of how God had pulled me through was inspiration for just a little bit of hope to break through into their lives.

I chose to believe there was purpose to my pain and I began to let this shape me. I hoped that it made me a better person, with more empathy and compassion, as well as giving me an ability to be better at relationships.

It was also during this time that I took part in the course *40 Days of Purpose* by Rick Warren (Grand Rapids, MI: Zondervan, 2003). The material helped to show me more of the bigger picture. It suggested that life on earth is a preparation for eternity. I liked that outlook. It made everything take on more meaning and purpose. I knew that whatever life threw at me, it would always have purpose, hope and destiny.

14

A Positive Shift

So, during the year 2005, released from the continual tide of going in and out of hospital, I started to feel as if I was actually part of something and living my life for a purpose. It was a year of making connections, trialling new things at church and having time to nurture and develop my young family.

I had reached a place of gratitude for all I had in my life, and I wanted to give thanks to God for all the strength, hope and promises he had given me. I didn't blame him for all that had happened, and there was a simple explanation for that. I believed it to be the work of Satan. God had not let me down, he had been faithful and had answered my prayers. My heart had grown, and despite the continuing needs of my children, I seemed to have a capacity to carry on giving.

Jasmine became a delight to me. After three years of anxiety and unknown outcomes, I was being rewarded as I watched her learn new skills. As a family, we learnt a simple sign language called Makaton which was a tool that helped her to learn to talk. She learnt to walk, she stopped wearing nappies during the day and she learnt to identify shapes. I loved to watch her turn a book around the right way when I had handed it to her upside down. It gave me great joy to see her absorbing the colours and pictures from her story books. Her engagement with life fascinated me. I loved to hear her squeal with delight when her sisters came near. I watched as she learnt new skills in slow motion. She learnt how to reach out to give a block to me, but it took more practise before she knew how to release it. This was a gift I had missed with Zoe and Georgia as they had speedily gained new skills unnoticed. Jasmine began to grasp things I never expected her to and she showed understanding in her responses. Her mastery of these different skills brought me a deep joy. I felt energized and alive. I could see that each day had the potential for something new, and motherhood became a fulfilling role once again.

I tried to organize my time and plan a schedule so I could spend quality time with each of the girls on their own at some point. Jasmine started nursery in a special-needs setting, a school with a department for early years. It catered for those with extreme learning delays and could also care for her gastrostomy and hydration needs. She continued having tea at Julie's once a week and this enabled me to spend time with Zoe and Georgia.

Georgia had settled well in school and was reported to be a 'lovely girl'; two simple words that made my heart soar with pride. Every little achievement filled me with happiness. The darkness of the previous years seemed a lot less gloomy from this perspective. Zoe's health was remarkably improved – she was now on medication for her problems with her thyroid, and her diabetes results were good overall, even though we often had a rollercoaster of daily readings. I loved the challenge of being their mum. I felt fulfilled in this role. I would have loved to have had more children, but I knew that my hands were full with our three girls, so Andy and I called it a day and decided to be grateful for our lot!

When I knew my family was complete and life became easier to manage, I decided to take some time to focus on me. Ever since my mid-teens, I had felt awkward about the size of my breasts. I was teased in school and I'd overheard the odd comment about how big they were. I decided that one day I would have a reduction. I felt like men would look at my chest rather than my face, and I certainly didn't feel feminine. By the time I'd had the children, my breasts were even bigger, my back was stooping and I had deep grooves in my shoulders from my bra straps. Now that I no longer needed to breastfeed, I knew that it was time to do something about this.

I had spoken to my doctor of this desire some years back, so I approached her again with my request. Fortunately, the NHS were able to cover the procedure, due to my size being so disproportionate to my body. I had hated this part of me for so long. It defined how I viewed myself, and it decided what kind of clothes I could wear. I felt ugly, frumpy and fat. It had even decided what wedding dress would look OK, twelve years previously. This was a big deal for me.

A week before the operation, in order to prepare myself, I thought I would watch a breast reduction operation on television. I found this very interesting, but it did make me question whether I should be doing this to myself. I prayed to God that if it wasn't right, he would show me. I didn't want anything to happen that would compromise family life again.

When the day arrived, I entered the ward with Andy, Zoe and Georgia. I was contemplative, excited, anxious and scared but I was 100 per cent sure I wanted this change. It was the day of my 33rd birthday and I was overwhelmed by loving cards with special words and thoughts from my friends and family. I couldn't express how grateful I was to God for such wonderful friends. I felt so special and loved.

As we ate birthday cake together, I glanced up, and there out of the window was a rainbow, full of colour. I felt God say to me, 'Believe, Emma; trust me. I love you.'

After my family had left, I introduced myself to Val, in the next bed. She was hoping to go home the next day after her tummy tuck operation, although she said she wasn't feeling very well, so she would have to wait and see. Night-time arrived, and sleep with it. I felt peaceful. Dawn broke, and my day of transformation was finally here. I prepared myself for the surgery and read as I waited. I was nervous but not anxious. When I arrived in the anaesthetic room, there was a rainbow painted on the wall!

When I awoke, I briefly wondered where I was and then, with feelings of relief, I realized I had survived. Once back on the ward, those initial feelings of relief disappeared and were replaced by fear – I was afraid that I was going to get an infection. Anxiety poured over me, drenching me like a flood, washing itself around the whole of my body. It was all-consuming and disabled my other senses.

In the midst of my worry, I was vaguely aware of Val in the bed next to me, even though she had hoped to go home. I stopped thinking about myself for a moment and began to listen to what was happening beside me. Val was in a bad way. Her wound had become infected and I could hear doctors asking for swabs and consent forms and who her next of kin was. She needed to go back to theatre to be opened up again so they could clean out the infection. They were with her for hours. She needed a lot of help, so I started to pray for her.

Over the next three days, I was consumed with worry and anxiety, not just for myself but for Val too. My heart would pound so loudly I could hear it in my ears. My hands and feet were cold and sweaty – I felt locked into anxiety. I asked God to save Val's life and to save me from an infection. The more I thought about infection, the more convinced I became that I was going to get one. I thought if I stayed awake day and night, I could stop an infection from happening. I was not in control of my thoughts – I had given the reins to fear. Anxiety had captured my simple concern and turned it into a towering monster that paralysed any thought of reason or reality. I had completely forgotten the two rainbows I had seen. I kept getting out of bed with my two wound drain bottles in a pillowcase and I spent two nights pacing up and down the corridor. I pleaded with God over and over, 'Please don't let me get an infection. Please heal Val.'

I rang my mum and told her of my extreme fears. She listened compassionately and told me she would pray for an angel to be guardian over me so I could switch off and go to sleep. I thanked her but wasn't sure how that was going to make any difference.

Later that day, my family came to visit. I had missed them – I felt a little guilty for being away from them and I was so pleased to see them. They helped me to focus on reality again. I was doing well and there were no signs of infection. Their visit was a gift to me and I was so grateful. After they had gone, I lay my head on the pillow and shut my eyes. As I lay there I began to hear singing – it seemed as if it was a chorus of people who were harmonizing. A feeling of peace washed over me as I listened to the words that were being repeated over and over: 'I am your guardian angel.' The contrast, fear to peace, was like dark to light and I soon fell asleep. When I awoke, I felt calm and refreshed, and the anxiety was gone.

I continued to heal and so did Val, slowly each day. I didn't get an infection. God took care of that. I wondered what would have happened with my anxiety had I not believed that God would help me.

This surgery transformed how I saw myself both inwardly and outwardly. It helped me to lay to rest the lies of ugliness that I had held in my mind. My confidence and self-image grew and I took more care of my appearance. I had had my hair cut very short, as it had been easier to manage, but I grew it longer and had it styled at the hairdressers. With my body in better proportion, I started to wear clothes that fitted me rather than jumpers two sizes too big, and for the first time in years I was able to wear a dress – finally both the top and bottom fitted! People complimented me and friends commented on the difference they saw in me. It felt like I'd turned from a caterpillar into a butterfly, and to top it all, I no longer suffered from such awful backache!

My surgery was followed by a relatively uneventful year – a time which we all welcomed with open arms. It was a relief to step back from the intensity of extra medical pressures on family life. A break from the storm. It was a time of refuelling, reflecting and refreshing. This time of rest was important as it wouldn't be long before the storm reappeared.

15

Health and Anxiety

Further issues with Zoe's thyroid were now coming to light. After a series of blood tests and medication changes, it became evident that she needed to have her thyroid gland taken out. Her thyroid would not stop producing too much thyroxine – her neck was very distended by the enormous gland and this made her feel very self-conscious. Her neck looked pregnant and her swallow had become uncomfortable.

We found ourselves back on familiar territory – Great Ormond Street. We were admitted to the same ward that Jasmine had been on when she had her gastrostomy.

In March 2008, when she was 11 years old, Zoe underwent six hours of surgery for a total thyroidectomy. It was a complicated procedure due to the size of the gland and its proportion to her neck. It was important that four small glands called parathyroid glands were preserved and retained from amongst the mass. Their function is to produce calcium and without them, Zoe would have had to have calcium supplements three times a day for the rest of her life. She didn't need that extra hassle along with the insulin she would always have to administer. The surgeon managed to maintain three of the four parathyroid glands, and Zoe's body was able to adjust to produce the right amount of calcium. The surgery was successful and for a year, she took one tablet each day and had her blood tested every three months. Zoe's replacement thyroxine tablets did their job. But by the end of that year, her thyroxine levels began to increase again, which meant readjusting her doses several times. This was an unusual outcome following a total thyroidectomy, so concern was expressed as to why Zoe was producing her own thyroxine again.

The year 2008 was another busy one. With everything else going on, we had also decided to extend our home. By the end of 2008, we were amazed to find that Jasmine had begun to master the art of swallowing fluids. It started while I was bathing her. We were playing with the cups and teapot in what I had seen as 'imaginative play', but Jasmine had other ideas as she promptly swallowed a whole cup of bathwater! This alerted me to reflect on the promise I had received in 2004, 'The gastrostomy will be temporary.' My excitement gathered, but I somehow needed to hold it at bay. I would need to use this moment as a marker of the beginning of a new journey. I knew there would be hurdles to jump and mountains to climb, but I held a sense of expectancy in my heart that this promise would be fulfilled.

Six months passed and they were full of activity. Zoe's diabetes control was fraught with challenges as we tried to keep her blood sugars in normal range. Jasmine's behaviour was becoming increasingly difficult to manage. In particular, the word 'no' was being used far too frequently, and quite often not even in context. We needed to be alert, patient, and ready with a creative action to support her.

I had also taken on the responsibility of leading a small group at church for discussion and connection time with friends. We met weekly with the purpose of encouraging each other.

We would spend time talking about how God interacted in our lives, and praying for each other. It was a time of growth and vulnerability for me. I wanted to do a good job leading, and for the most part I think I did OK, but I continued to battle with feelings of not being good enough.

My mind was a battlefield and I experienced anxiety over my health. I didn't want it to be this way, but I couldn't seem to stop the thoughts. When I was a teenager, I remember sitting on a coach during a school trip and thinking that I didn't want my mum to die. Now I had children of my own, my thoughts were bombarded with my own fears of dying and leaving them behind. I knew I should trust God and peace would be released, but I really struggled to do that.

The anxiety came upon me again when I felt a lump in the back of my throat. I went to the doctors to get it checked, but the doctor didn't seem to understand my concern and dismissed me. I went home frightened that if nothing was done, it would grow and then I would not be able to breathe and I would die. I began to wonder how long that process would take and how much time I had left. I was anxious and I hated it. Eventually, I went back to the doctor's and was reassured that all I could feel was my epiglottis which was perfectly normal. This helped with my anxiety for a few days, but it wasn't long before it returned. I was sure I could feel something extra in my throat.

My faith was challenged again. I truly believed God had promised me things, and I believed the many rainbows were a sign of these promises. I felt sure he had promised me that I would not have to experience the loss of a child again, but I struggled to have confidence in a faith without black-and-white evidence and proof that it worked. I wanted to know that I was going to be OK and have a long and satisfying life. I wanted faith that came with a guarantee!

My irrational thoughts led me into a torturous place. I had my funeral planned. I was going to record a voice memo for everyone I was leaving behind; I was going to write letters to Andy and the girls, telling them of my love, with words of advice and encouragement. I made contact and spent time with old friends, privately believing that this was the last time I would speak to them. I was unable to eat and imagined cancerous growths all over my body. I was terrified and wound up like a coiled spring.

Life continued around me, but I was disengaged. One afternoon, Zoe asked, 'Are you OK, Mum? You don't seem yourself.'

'I'm not coping. I think I'm dying.' The words were out before I could stop them.

'Why do you think that?'

'I think I have throat cancer and it has spread all over my body.'

'And what evidence do you have that this is true?' she said.

I didn't have any evidence. I felt awful that I had burdened her with my fears. How could I have done that to her? I was surprised at her response, 'Mum, you will be OK. Stop worrying!' My young daughter was so rational and mature!

The following day, I was still in a state of extreme anxiety. I tried to go through the motions of pretending I was OK, but in truth, I wasn't very good at it. We had travelled over to my parents' house earlier that day, and my mum picked up that I wasn't doing so well. I was able to have some time alone with her, and this helped me to be more grounded and rational. In the afternoon, Jasmine wanted to go to a park with a lake, and although the weather didn't look great, everyone decided to go along. As we arrived, it started to rain, but undeterred, we all bundled out of the car and went for a walk. Zoe and I lagged behind the others, and as we chatted, we both glanced over the lake to a hue of rainbow colours. It was there for a few seconds, and then it was gone.

Zoe turned to me. 'There you are, Mum. I prayed for that yesterday. You're going to be fine!'

I went to the doctor again about my throat. There was inflammation but it was due to acid reflux, not a growth of any kind. I was healthy. I was not going to die of anything, and I had just put myself through a storm of doubt and fear that had been horrible. I was disappointed in myself for not trusting that God had good plans for me.

Another six months had passed and life was full of appointments – blood tests for Jasmine and Zoe, both of whom now had thyroid issues, and Georgia had ongoing ENT appointments for hearing loss and recurring infections. Andy was away on business quite a lot and life continued to be much more stressful than I would have liked. Zoe was waiting for an MRI scan to investigate where the extra thyroxine was coming from. The scan revealed two small areas of active thyroid tissue! The parathyroid glands must have retained some minute thyroid cells around them which had begun to multiply all over again. The consultant said it was an 'unusual outcome'. He had only seen one other case like this in his thirty years of experience. They continued to monitor Zoe and, over time, she came off all supplemented tablets and was able to produce the right amount of thyroxine independent of medical support or intervention. I thought this was miraculous!

I was trying to be victorious in my positive thoughts, but it was a constant battle for me. It was during these investigations about Zoe's health that God spoke to me again.

This time, I heard him very clearly.

16

Another Promise Fulfilled

It was midnight and the household had closed down for the night. We had all gone to bed early, worn out from the day. Everyone was asleep in their own beds and I stirred to Zoe's whispering voice beside me: 'I'm hypo.' This meant she had low blood sugars and needed some sugar. I couldn't quite rouse myself and I heard her voice again, 'I'm hypo.' I opened my eyes and reached out in the dark. She was not there! I nudged Andy and asked him to go and check her blood sugars. When Andy went to check on her she was sound asleep and had definitely not been at my bedside a few moments before. However, she was hypo. Andy woke her and dealt with it straightaway.

I chose to believe that God used Zoe's voice, a gentle whisper in the night, to get my attention and show me that I had no cause to be anxious, that he was in control and was watching over us, protecting us from harm. At this time, I chose to stop worrying about Zoe's health. I also chose to believe that I would remain well and healthy. This was a turning point for me. Whenever a bad thought came, if it was without physical symptoms, I told myself, 'No, Emma, God said it's going to be OK. Stop it!' Then I would thank God for my health. These choices and thoughts worked well for me and I experienced a freedom from anxiety in my mind for longer periods of time.

In 2010, Andy turned 40 and we all went away for three weeks to celebrate. The first stop was to Toronto in Canada to stay with his sister, her husband and two boys. The distance between us meant that we didn't get to see each other that often, so we packed in a tight schedule of outings to maximize our time together. One of the activities was crazy golf at the local golf club. The course was fun and manageable for all of us, so we all got involved in playing the game.

After a while, we were thirsty and ready for a drink. The nearest café was a short walk away and en route we passed a number of parked golf buggies. These caught Jasmine's attention and she expressed her wish to ride in one, but they weren't on offer to crazy golfers like us. Jasmine's limited understanding meant that she couldn't comprehend this concept, and I thought I would distract her attention by getting her an ice cream. This worked – for a short while. She devoured her ice cream very happily but didn't stay still long enough for me to give her water, and before everyone else had finished, she was up and away, ready for the next adventure. Jasmine characteristically walked with her head down looking at her feet and she didn't have much of a sense of direction, but this time she had a goal – the golf buggy was calling her!

Jasmine and I left the others behind us and as we rounded the corner, there they were – a collection of parked buggies all waiting for their next customers. Also in this courtyard were some staff unloading goods for the café, and I thought it would be worth asking them if Jasmine could at least sit in one of the buggies. It would be a good opportunity for me to give Jasmine her water via her gastrostomy as she sat there pretending to play cars.

The staff were agreeable to the idea and I was grateful they were, as Jasmine was already halfway in! She wriggled over to the passenger side, so I quickly attached the plastic tubing to her gastrostomy button and began to pour the water into the top of the tube. Always alert to Jasmine moving about while pouring water into her, I loosely held the tube up ready for movement and was right to do so, as she decided to move over to the driver's side. She grasped the steering wheel in her chubby little hands, smiled, and let out an excited squeal. Bouncing up and down, her foot hit the accelerator pedal. Suddenly, we were off! The buggy had been left with keys in it. The water tube splashed out of my hand as I let it go. The buggy raced headlong into the wall of the flowerbed just ahead of us, gathering enough momentum for it to knock the wall down. Jasmine was unharmed and quite oblivious to the chaos around her. At that moment, the others came around the corner from the café and took in the scene before them. Embarrassed, we apologized to the staff members, and gave our details in case we had to pay for damages. We left promptly, stifling giggles.

We also had an eventful trip to New York. We were travelling first class in a train, where we were entertained by a lady who was very friendly, but kept saying strange things. We had no idea at the time that she shouldn't have been travelling and was most likely suffering with dementia. She was removed from the train as we crossed the Canadian-American border. New York really was the city that never sleeps and we loved it. As we ended our time there, we phoned to order a cab to take us to the airport. We thought it was very expensive, but assumed that this was just how much things cost in New York. When our vehicle arrived, it turned out we had booked a stretch limousine! We felt like royalty and enjoyed every moment.

Barbados was our third and final destination. Here we enjoyed family time in the swimming pool, unlimited cocktails and, in particular, we loved the Caesar salad. We had an amazing opportunity to swim with turtles too. It was a very special family holiday.

September 2010 saw the beginning of a new school year for the girls. For Jasmine, this was to be a year of change too, as she transitioned from being given water through her gastrostomy to being allowed to swallow her fluids orally, in school as well as at home. Having already established her ability to drink at home for some time, this was an easy adaptation for her, but it was not so easy for her teachers, who were bound by health and safety regulations.

My requests for her to be allowed to drink normally at school had been denied because of her medical reports. I found this frustrating, but I was ready to confront any obstacles in our way. I had fought for my girl before and been successful, so I wasn't going to sit back and accept this.

I called a meeting at the school with the speech and language team, the community paediatrician, staff on the leadership of the school and our social worker. I thought at least someone in the room would back my request and help us win the right for Jasmine to drink freely at school, as she was doing at home. I wanted this gastrostomy gone and I had enough faith to push hard. I prayed that something would be released within this tight system – a system which rightly wanted to avoid errors but, in my opinion, had lost something of a common-sense approach.

I was asked to open the meeting and to explain the reason for my request and the history behind it. I must have sounded crazy as I told them how I had given my daughter toast. I talked of the rainbows and how I believed that God was going to fulfil his promise to heal Jasmine's neurological disorder. I held nothing back and I hoped I would be taken seriously. I shared how we had been allowing Jasmine to drink from a cup and how I had monitored her for signs of aspiration, like eye tearing, coughing or chest infections and that we had seen no evidence of these since we had been letting her drink at home.

The outcome of the meeting, after some awkward discussions, was to refer us to a specialist in London. I was relieved that the door had not been closed on the subject, but that my insistence had led them to seek higher authority on the matter. I felt a peace upon me as we waited for the appointment to come through, but I'm glad it didn't take too long. The speech and language therapist from school met us at the appointment, and I felt suspicious that she had been sent to check that we would tell the right story. I wondered what may have been said about me after we left the meeting, but I concluded that it was good the school were taking my request seriously.

From my perspective, this appointment couldn't have gone better. Andy and I were listened to and our thoughts and opinions were taken on board. Jasmine engaged well and showed them how she could swallow from various different cups and in different positions and it was agreed that we could go on a six-month trial at school. There were conditions to follow and it was agreed that if after six months it was a success, Jasmine could have her gastrostomy taken out.

I was elated. I wanted to celebrate all that Jasmine had overcome despite the 'stumbling blocks' which could so easily have robbed her of her quality of life. We went to a pizza restaurant to celebrate, and Jasmine was allowed as many fizzy drinks as she liked.

Our six-month trial ended with the outcome I had been longing for. Seven years, almost to the date after I had seen that rainbow though my car windscreen, Jasmine had her gastrostomy sewn up. We were overjoyed and thanked God for his faithfulness to us.

17

Autism?

Mothering the three girls made for interesting times. They were all unique and in different stages of development, so they needed different things from me. It was 2011 and Zoe was 14, Georgia 11 and Jasmine 8. I had felt nervous of the teenage years, as I had heard so many stories of teenagers being diffi-cult to manage and I wasn't sure I felt equipped for that, but Zoe was easy for us so far, and I was thankful that I had a great relationship with her. I had been fairly strict as I parented the girls, particularly Zoe and Jasmine, as they had seemed to push the boundaries harder. I had a very close bond with Zoe, and I would discuss life's mysteries with her as I had tried to make sense of all that was going on in my world. She would engage with me on deep levels and showed maturity beyond her years. In disciplining her, I would reason with her and discuss what had happened and how we could respond to it. She wanted to know 'why' from an early age, and having clear boundaries of what I expected from her seemed to work well. Georgia was different, she was much quieter and rarely needed a cross word; she desired to please and was compliant in many ways. Given the health needs and personalities of Zoe and Jasmine, there were many occasions when Georgia blended into the background. I was aware of this, along with the 'middle child' phenomenon, so I tried to allocate time just for the two of us.

Now that the girls were older, I was grateful that everyone had better health and I was no longer looking over my shoulder for the next hospital stay. Jasmine was developing well and most of her speech could be understood by people who knew her. Her special school was an excellent place for learning, and she was thriving there. We were also fortunate to have a very good network of people around us. I had excellent relationships with our social worker, specialist behaviour nurse and the local charity White Lodge who supplied us with brilliant care workers. My friends were invaluable to me. In addition, we were very blessed to have a number of special play schemes in our area which provided fun days out for Jasmine in the school holidays; this meant I was able to have some quality time with Zoe and Georgia. Overall, life was good, but there were two things in particular that I was struggling with; one was my marriage, and the other was Jasmine's behaviour.

Family life was diverse and the needs of our daughters had taken over my thought life and zapped my energy levels. I found it hard to engage with my wifely role as well as be a mother to my girls. Andy would get the 'tired Emma' at the end of the day, which wasn't particularly satisfying for him or for me, and our conversations would often result in frustrated misunderstandings. We were struggling. All that had happened to us was having an obvious effect on our relationship. We had both dealt with our losses in very different ways and because of the continual strain of family life, we had prioritized the girls above each other. Andy worked to earn money and I brought up the children and kept the house going, amongst other things. Our marriage was not particularly enjoyable, but it functioned for the sake of the family.

On top of this, Jasmine's behaviour confused me. The parenting methods I had used with Zoe and Georgia didn't seem to work for her, so I was challenged to know how best to parent her. Her first word had been 'no' and it seemed to be part of every sentence she had used since then. Sometimes her 'no' would really mean 'yes' and this made it difficult to ascertain what her desire was. One 'no' that was clear, however, was her refusal to do as she was asked. I found her responses to what I considered reasonable requests very confusing. Her defiant reaction to simple requests such as, 'Please put your shoes on, we are going out' and her aggression towards us in response to this was difficult to handle. By the age of 9, she was intellectually scoring levels which put her between 4 and 5 years, but these outbursts looked more like a 2-year-old's tantrums. Simple daily tasks, like getting out of bed, washing, going to the toilet, getting dressed, having breakfast, taking a drink, putting shoes on and leaving the house proved challenging, as we would be met with refusal after refusal.

For a couple of years I had been puzzled by Jasmine's behavioural outbursts, as they seemed so random in their presentation. Her mood would change rapidly and often with no obvious triggers. One minute she would be happy, then within seconds, she would become angry or sad. One trigger we had noted was her problem with transitions. Jasmine struggled with moving from one task to another and from one place to another at home and at school. One example was her refusal to leave the house and get on the school bus. Through a process of trial and error, and with professional support and special education, we had learnt certain strategies to manage this, but we hadn't been able to eliminate the problem.

Jasmine's behaviour had become very controlling. Her world was all about her, and she was demanding and receiving vast amounts of attention, yet nothing seemed to satisfy her hunger for it. She would follow me around within 30cm, even if I was just going to the toilet. She would demand I play with her, then shove or pinch me if I didn't obey her request. She was growing in size now too, so it wasn't so easy to move her away. Sometimes, I would lock myself in the downstairs toilet just for a bit of space, even if the door was being kicked on the other side! Jasmine was also unable to entertain herself, which made her even more demanding.

I believed that Jasmine needed consistency and boundaries. Given that her understanding was limited, I thought that if I made it clear what was expected of her, she would be able to learn a model to help her cope with life's uncertainties. The very essence of a tight-boundaried model, however, rather than settling her down, seemed to bring about an increase of refusals and inappropriate noes. I tried to think of things to positively reward her good choices, but there were very few things that she wanted enough to motivate her. Stickers, an obvious choice for her developmental age, only worked occasionally, and it seemed that praise of any kind would be met with opposition. We tried chocolate rewards which she would throw on the floor, and even had a prize box for good choice-making, but with little effect. I found it difficult to notice good choices – everything seemed to be a battle. Jasmine wouldn't walk very far and, even though she could walk short distances, she would often sit down on the ground without any warning and refuse to get up. One time, she sat on the ground for twenty minutes until she decided to move. When she was small, we could pick her up and carry her, but as she got bigger this wasn't possible, and if we tried to force her, we would be pinched, scratched, hit, or spat on. We soon got the message that a hands-off approach was needed. On the occasions she was walking nicely,

I would try to seize the moment and say to her, 'Lovely walking, Jasmine, well done!' But her response would be to sit down and refuse to get up!

We were perplexed as to why she was responding like this. As time went on, I could see these responses becoming entrenched. It was upsetting for her and incredibly difficult for us to work with as parents. I searched for answers to solve the problems. I wondered if I could sort it out by using punishment instead. I had learnt about the process of conditioning during my years of training as a nurse. An idea came to me that if I put a hot sauce on her tongue each time she said 'no', she would associate the word with an unpleasant experience and then maybe she would stop saying it. Although controversial, this tactic produced a result. It worked and she even asked if we could bring the sauce with us wherever we went! It seemed to comfort her to have a boundary, and it helped her to comply. I would observe her talking to herself about saying 'yes' because she didn't like the sauce. Consequently, she was being more obedient, and I rarely had to put the sauce on her tongue.

I was relieved, but there was tension between Andy and me as he didn't agree with my technique. While I was being consistent, our parenting was out of kilter, and this didn't help Jasmine or anyone else who had to listen to our disagreements. Family life was strained. If I didn't use the sauce, Jasmine would say 'no', and if I did use the sauce, Andy would be upset. I didn't know what to do. I didn't like the sauce idea much either, but when I was weighing it against the risk of Jasmine becoming dehydrated because she refused to drink, I thought it was the better of two evils.

Some months passed using this technique, and although I rarely had to fight Jasmine to get the sauce on her tongue, there were occasions when I did and I felt terrible. I felt like I was bullying her, but I didn't know how else to get her to comply with demands that I believed were in her best interests.

On our next visit with the social worker, she asked me how things were going.

'It's really hard to manage Jasmine,' I said. 'She says "no" to so many things, and I had this idea that if I put spicy sauce on her tongue, she would associate saying "no" with something unpleasant.' I continued, 'She responds very well to it. She even asks to take it out with her. The only thing is, Andy doesn't agree with it, and I can see why.'

Unsurprisingly, the social worker wasn't very happy with this method either! She decided to bring in a behaviour support nurse to help us make life work better. Waiting lists were long, but they found a way, and we were seen within a month. This visit was both helpful and frustrating for me. I was told that I needed to stop using negative consequence parenting as this wasn't helping matters. I think I already knew this, but the positive rewards model had not been successful either.

The nurse made up some laminated sheets of pictures of various tasks. Some of the pictures had Velcro on the back so we could move them about, depending on the order of the activity Jasmine would do first. I could present them to her, and she would see clearly what was wanted. We talked together about the things that would motivate Jasmine to do as she was asked, and we came to the realization that I was the most rewarding thing to her, rather than any material item. Her positive rewards were very limited as I wasn't always available on her demand, and I didn't want to always be at her beck and call.

These sheets worked for a while; Jasmine enjoyed taking the pictures on and off the laminated sheets and rearranging them, but this wasn't helpful when I wanted her to get on with the task, as she just wanted to play with the pictures. In the end, they became a nuisance rather than a help.

We also discovered that we could give Jasmine options such as, 'Do you want this or do you want that?' We would sometimes get a positive outcome from this. It wasn't until later that I realized I needed to try to present her with two positive options rather than one positive and one negative, which obviously gave us a fifty-fifty chance of ending up with a negative outcome. It was so hard to identify what Jasmine actually wanted because of her confusion and overuse of the word 'no'.

We tried numerous disciplines and techniques to manage her, from punishment and negative consequences to bribery and rewards and back round again. Each of these worked for a period of time, but none of them established a new pattern of compliance.

Things began to worsen rather than improve. I felt that the methods the nurse had given us were not motivating for Jasmine. I thought there must be a reason for all of this and, in that, a solution. In asking these questions, we were sent to the local team of paediatricians, who carried out a number of assessments, which led them to diagnose attention deficit hyperactivity disorder (ADHD) and oppositional defiant disorder (ODD). We had the option of medication for the ADHD, but the ODD was more about strategies in managing behaviours. This was something we had already been investing our ideas and energies into with little effect, so it was hard to hear.

I embraced the idea of medication. We needed something that would help Jasmine. However, I wasn't totally convinced that ADHD was a correct diagnosis and I challenged this a number of times. So much so, that the paediatrician sent us to a London hospital to see a specialist in challenging behaviour. I wondered by this point if Jasmine was autistic. I had noticed a number of behaviours that I had seen in people diagnosed with autism spectrum disorder, so this would explain a number of things. In the end, I found the outcome of this appointment very disappointing. They did think she had ADHD and they thought she had extreme ODD rather just the simple form! They said she didn't present enough characteristics of autism. They promised they would get a local team on board to support us more, which was in fact a referral back to the specialist behaviour nurses whom we had met a while before.

The nurse was very supportive and offered more positive strategies that I could use, but I had yet to be convinced that they would actually work. It was at this time, together with the nurse, that I became aware of the role of anxiety that was present for Jasmine. I had heard of a condition called pathological demand avoidance (PDA), which causes the person to have extreme anxiety whenever a demand is placed upon them. It wasn't a well-known condition, nor was it recognized by the diagnostic manuals for medical conditions. However, there was a website (www.pdasociety.org.uk) that explained it and as I read through the pages, it was like someone had written an article about Jasmine. I was certain that this was what we were dealing with, so we decided to revisit the specialists with this new information to see if we could get a diagnosis of PDA.

It was a difficult day. Andy and I travelled by train, with Jasmine in her wheelchair. The previous trip had been difficult too as she had sat down on the pavement on the way and refused to walk for what seemed like a long time, and then she refused to leave the appointment and sat in the stairwell of the hospital until we could persuade her to come with us. Cautious because of this previous experience, we decided to take the wheelchair this time.

As we left the station, we told Jasmine that we would just pick up a coffee on our way to the appointment, as we thought it was important for her to know what was happening. As we approached the coffee shop inside the hospital, and Andy went in to get our drinks, she began to shout, 'No, I don't want you to!'

I couldn't see what her problem was; we weren't making her have a coffee! In her anger that we didn't obey her, she looked at my hands on the wheelchair and began to scrape her nails across them. She squirmed furiously in her seat and continued to shout. Embarrassed by her behaviour, I ignored the scratching as best I could and marched her wheelchair beyond the coffee shop as if I was taking her straight to the appointment room. She was clearly very distressed by this, but I just couldn't see why. I paced up and down the corridor for a while, until Andy caught up with us and she seemed to settle down again. Needless to say, we arrived at the appointment a little flustered.

Jasmine was interviewed by the team and we were questioned about how life was for us. In light of the aggressive outbursts, it was decided to trial a medication that should help to reduce these. I questioned autism with the team again and was told that while she had a number of traits of autism, her social interaction was too engaging to qualify for this label. I was intent on finding a reason for her unreasonable outbursts. I wasn't satisfied with their answers and they didn't even want to acknowledge the existence of PDA!

We decided we would trial Jasmine on the anti-aggression medication after we dealt with another very public meltdown in London. It was impossible to reason with her when she was stressed. In fact, if we were within reach, she would kick, spit, shout and scratch. It was painful and embarrassing when we were out in public. It also caused tension between Andy and me, as he would want to try to stop her, which would often mean he got hurt, whereas I would leave her and move back a few paces so I could see her but she couldn't hurt me. I didn't know what Andy was thinking, but assumed that he thought I didn't care and that I should be able to deal with it. I felt powerless and it made me sad each time it happened. I thought he should stand back, as I believed the interaction and questioning of what the matter was actually made it worse. We were both cross with each other about how we were dealing with the situation.

Life was tough. Even getting Jasmine's new medication was a challenge. The GP wouldn't prescribe it, as it wasn't licensed in children so young. The London hospital couldn't give it to us because we were out of area and the local hospital couldn't prescribe it for more than one month at a time due to their budget! Our behaviour nurse was brilliant and got us a referral to the local Child and Adolescent Mental Health Services (CAMHS) department. We had to go on a waiting list.

We had another hurdle to jump. In the process of gathering information, it was noticed by Jasmine's school that she seemed quite flat and depressed. The anti-aggression medication was expensive, so the psychiatrist decided to try an antidepressant medication instead. This seemed to make no difference, so we increased the dose. This was a huge mistake.

It was the beginning of May 2012 and Jasmine's birthday was at the end of the week. She had spotted a waterpark in Blackpool on TV and decided that she wanted to go there for her birthday. So we had booked a hotel and got tickets to the pool. Jasmine seemed very excited. For the previous couple of weeks, we had experienced some new issues with Jasmine undoing her seatbelt and standing up on her seat on the school bus. This was obviously not acceptable, and I was being pressed by the transport team and the school to put her in a Houdini harness to prevent her from doing this. She would be strapped in until an adult released her. I was against this idea, as I saw it as taking a backward step from the progress she had made in sitting more independently. However, I could see this was an issue that needed to be addressed.

The transport team had given some grace to Jasmine, as they had stopped the bus until she was strapped in again, but it wasn't fair on the other children. So after a few days of this, they refused to take her into school until we could sort it out. I wasn't very happy with her! Her school was a fair distance away, and over the next few days, I drove her there. The rule was that she would sit in the back, no music and no talking. I needed her to understand that this wasn't acceptable and I didn't want her to think that I would be taking her to school now, instead of the bus. After a week of this routine, I asked if we could trial her on the bus again. She seemed to understand that she should keep her seatbelt on.

Jasmine managed one successful day before I got a distressed phone call from school. On her way in on that particular morning, she had attacked the lovely lady who was her bus escort. Lynne would sit in the back with the children, supervising them, singing, making jokes and telling stories. She was a wonderful, happy woman. Jasmine had started well and stayed in the confines of her seatbelt, but had stood up with it still on, turned around and whacked Lynne, pulled her hair and scratched her. Although Jasmine could behave like this, it was usually if we had asked her to do something. Lynne was clearly shaken up.

I was summoned to collect Jasmine from school at the end of the day, as she was not welcome on the school bus. I was ashamed of her and I felt awful about what she had done, so I found Lynne, gave her some flowers and said sorry to her. I felt a burden of responsibility.

My instincts told me something wasn't right with Jasmine – the intensity of aggression had ratcheted itself up since increasing her medication. I decided not to give her any more of the antidepressant medication so I rang the CAMHS team and got them to agree for me to take her off it. The problem was, this took us back to square one. We still had the issue of aggression, but now we had no medication for it.

We decided we couldn't do Jasmine's birthday trip, so we cancelled our hotel and trip to the waterpark. Jasmine was too volatile, we couldn't take the risk of more public humiliation. It was so sad seeing her growling, 'don't sing happy birthday to me' as she ripped the wrapping paper off her birthday presents. Her day at school was difficult too and the class were unable to sing to her and share her cake. She returned at the end of the day with her birthday cake just as I had sent it in that morning. This was hard to witness and it hurt to know how distressed she must have been feeling. After this incident, Jasmine was prescribed medication that was to reduce the aggressive outbursts. Thankfully, this worked and life improved somewhat.

Things had changed within the CAMHS team and we were assigned a new psychiatrist. I began to ask her about autism and, after her doing some more questionnaires, it was finally accepted that Jasmine ticked enough boxes to indicate autism.

I was a little relieved that we had some reasons for her confusing behaviour, and it helped me to see why she was different to some of her peers with Down's syndrome. On the other hand, the more I read about autism, the more I could see that something still didn't quite fit. I was sure we were missing something. Her social skills weren't the classically documented ones you would expect of someone with autism. She would demand unhealthy amounts of time with people, and manipulate what she wanted out of the situation. Particularly with me. She would demand that I be by her side while undertaking a task, but then if I asked her to do anything she would bow her head, lock herself down and refuse to engage with me. If I walked away she would crumple to the floor or kick out and trash the room. I couldn't win, and it was so frustrating. We tried lists, games, jokes, challenges, different family members helping her. Sometimes these strategies would work and sometimes they wouldn't.

She would also struggle with greeting people if she hadn't initiated the first interaction. However, if she had initiated it, she was overfriendly and would often say, 'Hello, smelly' to whoever she was speaking to! While she presented some very confusing behaviours that weren't the standard behaviours of autism or of a learning disability, she also had many behaviours that fitted with these diagnoses. I found myself feeling perplexed – a lot – and struggling to accept Jasmine. She was my daughter, and I knew I should love her despite her behaviour, but it was hard.

18

Unconditional Love

There have been times when I have wanted the complications of my life to disappear. This included thinking that if I were to send Jasmine away, life would be so much easier. It wasn't a comfortable place to be, but that was the truth. I thought before my mothering journey began that I would be able to love unconditionally; I believed I would adore my children no matter what. I thought I'd got the acceptance thing sorted. Of course, I was shocked about Jasmine having Down's syndrome when she was born and wondered if I would be able to manage, but once I'd got over that, I embraced the fact that she was mine and whether I liked what was going on for her or me, I was her mum and always would be.

I felt like I had accepted Jasmine for who she was; in fact, it had even crossed my mind to adopt another child with Down's syndrome when Jasmine was 4 or 5 because she was so lovely. She was very cute when she was small. I loved to see her sit and babble, grin widely and giggle. She used to delight in watching her sisters play around her. Once we had got over the hurdle of being nil by mouth, she loved to eat, and she slowly grasped new skills, which would bring great joy to me. She truly was a blessing to our family, and my world was richer for having her in it. I was surprised that as she got older, I began to feel as if I was rejecting her.

As Jasmine's behaviour got harder to manage, I started to battle with my feelings towards her and the situations that arose because of her actions. I had tried so hard to 'fix' her with various parenting methods, and yet I hadn't been able to stop the refusals and outbursts. Maybe they had even made the behaviours worse? I really didn't know what to do with her, and I wasn't sure how to react to her any more. I had probably been sending silent rejection vibes, and maybe this was making her worse. It all seemed so complex, I didn't understand or know what to do.

I found myself seeking sympathy from friends. I would go into great detail about a difficult encounter in order to earn a response such as, 'It's so difficult for you!'; 'I don't know how you do it!'; 'You're amazing and you always seem to have a smile on your face!' Conversations like this would help me feel rewarded for my efforts and energize me to keep going. However, I later learnt that this was also confirming to me that life was difficult and that Jasmine was a massive challenge. I found myself feeling negative towards her as I made complaint after complaint about her.

One evening Zoe challenged me: 'Stop talking about how difficult it is. It doesn't change anything and it just makes you feel stressed. The more you talk about it, the bigger it feels to you.' I was a little taken aback by what she said – this was not the affirming response I had grown used to! But her words had a powerful impact on me. I began to make a conscious effort to limit these types of conversations, and sure enough, I began to feel happier and more positive. I started to believe that one day it would get better, and I began to see how caring, helpful and funny Jasmine was.

I would often look at Jasmine's face and think, 'She is so different.' This seemed significant to me in both positive and

negative ways. I had seen miracles occur because of her existence and needs, which was amazing. On the other hand, the
media seemed to be telling me that she was an unwanted person because she had Down's syndrome. I felt like I was in a
debate for and against my own child. It all seemed inhumane
and unmotherly. Was Jasmine really so unacceptable? Was she
not good enough or intelligent enough or pretty enough? I felt
guilty about my lack of acceptance of her, and I was reminded
of the hurt I had felt when I was young, when I had been called
ugly, and how I hadn't felt accepted. I knew I had to fight this
for the sake of my child.

The fact that Jasmine had Down's syndrome didn't define
her. It may have described her facial features and given a reason for her learning difficulties, but it certainly didn't describe
her personality. I had heard that people with Down's syndrome
were loving, happy, affectionate and stubborn. Jasmine could
be all of these things, but what this label didn't describe was
that she could swing from deliriously happy one moment to
sad or angry the next moment. She didn't like being touched,
so cuddles, affection and love were only available if she gave
permission for them. She was shy and reserved and seemed to
panic if she was required to greet anyone. That wasn't my idea
of someone with Down's syndrome. I had naively thought that
people with Down's syndrome were extroverts, always on the
hunt for fun and interaction with anyone who would laugh
with them.

My daughter was unique. I began to think that her autism
described her better than her Down's syndrome. However, de-
scribing her wasn't high on my list of priorities. I needed to love
her unconditionally and equip her for life. I wanted to mother
her in the way she needed me to, and I found that in order
to do this, I had to sacrifice a lot of my own needs. It was a

challenge to love unconditionally! It was easy to love when the conditions were favourable and the person receiving the love was compliant and behaving satisfactorily, but I found it a lot harder when my love was being rejected.

It was February 2013 and it was bedtime in the Rutland household – well, bedtime for Jasmine, anyway! Andy was away on business, and I was tired. This wasn't a helpful place in which to start the hair-washing and bedtime routine, but this is how it was and I had to just get on with it. Jasmine wanted to use Zoe's en suite shower on this particular evening, and as Zoe was home, we consulted her and she agreed as she sat on her bed looking at her phone.

After some discussion about the temperature of the water, Jasmine entered the shower cubicle. After more persuasion, she agreed to get her hair wet. Still unable to wash her own hair, she needed me to apply the correct amount of shampoo as she liked to squeeze the whole bottle until it was empty! I knew she didn't like getting it in her eyes, and she liked the flannel to be arranged in a particular way before she would put it over her face, so I arranged it for her with meticulous precision. I was a little irritated by this, to be truthful, as I couldn't see the need to waste time on such a task, but I did it anyway. Finally, Jasmine allowed me to put the shampoo on her hair, but I was stopped short as she began to shout, 'Stop! No! Go away!' It may have seemed a trivial thing, but I snapped. I was driven by my determination to complete the job I'd started, and my hands were clamped tight around her hair. On realizing that she was trapped in my fingers, Jasmine kicked me. I was angry with her and with the situation yet again. I kicked her back and told her, 'I'm washing your hair!' I could feel rage bubbling within me as Zoe came to the rescue and ushered me away. I was ashamed. I was broken.

What kind of behaviour was that? How could I carry on looking after her? I knew something had to change.

After a broken night's sleep, I picked up the phone and rang our social worker. She was a kind, caring lady and I trusted her. I told her what had happened the night before and asked her if there was any way she could take Jasmine away, even if it was for a short while, so I could recover and rebuild my strength. There was no instant solution to my request, but our conversation did lead to us accessing once-a-month respite care. It took a while to establish, as we had to find the right family and train them to look after her.

The social worker's immediate response was to advise me to stay out of Jasmine's way and for Andy to do all the personal caring and discipline. Fortunately, he had returned late that evening, so this kept us going for a few days. Not long after this, it all went wrong again. Jasmine had insisted on getting a hot pizza out of the oven, after being told to wait. The incident ended up with her spitting in Andy's face and him losing his temper with her. Andy and I felt as if we were lost at sea with no compass to guide us. The waves were lashing over us and we thought we were going to drown. Our boat was coming apart and starting to sink.

Andy went to church the next morning with Zoe and Georgia. Feeling fragile, I stayed at home with Jasmine. I was unsure of what might happen next but, in the end, we had a nice morning pulling out all the recycling bottles and tubs for junk modelling. Andy returned with a fresh look about him. At church, the prayer team had taken some time with him and had asked God for strength to carry on. I had my turn to go to church in the evening, and I took my opportunity to speak to the prayer team. I told them what had been happening from my perspective, as they already had some idea from what Andy had said earlier in the day. I was feeling so anxious about what we were going to do with Jasmine. As they prayed, my knees began to shake uncontrollably and at the same time, I felt a peace wash over me. My breathing slowed and I felt renewed. One of the prayers indicated that the fruits of the Spirit were key to our survival. These are 'love, joy, peace, patience, kindness, goodness, faithfulness, gentleness, [and] self-control' (Gal. 5:22,23, RSV). They are spiritual gifts from God which can help us to live life better. I came away from church a little spaced out but feeling much less traumatized.

Quite often, when Jasmine had a meltdown, it would leave me feeling stunned. I would find it hard to focus on anything and I would feel fragile for several days. The day after church, I woke with new strength and a fresh hope that life would improve. An idea came to me that I should make nine posters with Jasmine, each representing a fruit of the Spirit. We decided to write a word a day and then decorate the page with more words and stickers about what it might mean to Jasmine. She enjoyed the interaction and colouring exercise. We displayed our artwork on the fridge for all to see, and this made for interesting conversations as people came to visit us.

As we went through the week, we found that each of the fruits overlapped with one another. Patience meant waiting with self-control. Kindness supports another person. Gentleness was a way of expressing kindness. Faithfulness is about sticking together even when it's hard to do that. As we talked about them and incorporated them into our language to guide Jasmine, we discovered that they were more than words, they carried power. We began to see Jasmine act out more gentleness, try to exercise self-control and to smile after tears. We saw goodness when she said, 'OK, Mummy' when she felt like saying 'no'. She even came home from school one day singing a rap about patience!

She continued to struggle when we asked her to do anything and found it hard when we said 'no' to her but we saw an improvement. Even I seemed to be more resilient and stayed calm when she would refuse to do something.

A year passed by and our patience and new techniques had improved life with Jasmine, but I still had some niggling questions about what was causing her responses to simple requests like, 'Finish your drink.' I found my attention being drawn back to PDA and I began to do some research. I found there was a centre in Nottingham, UK – the Elizabeth Newson Centre – which was a hub of resource for information, diagnostic tools and support. I learnt that PDA was not yet recognized as a formal condition in the health diagnostic manuals, and therefore it was not easy to find a professional who would diagnose it. However, it did have recognition by The National Autistic Society. I found a number of resources via the internet and I sent off for a book called *Understanding Pathological Demand Avoidance Syndrome in Children* by Phil Christie, Margaret Duncan, Zara Healy and Ruth Fidler (London: Jessica Kingsley Publishers, 2011).

As I read, it was like someone had written a book about my child without using her name! It answered many of my questions and gave me revelation about how Jasmine saw the world around her. If this was right, Jasmine was not being deliberately defiant or disobedient, she was experiencing extreme anxiety levels whenever she sensed a demand was being put upon her. I had no idea that asking her to have a drink or put her coat on could cause anxiety. I began to understand why she would want to avoid demands if they were making her feel so awful.

Initially, I was relieved – I had finally found some answers – but as this new information began to sink in, I experienced a number of emotions, from relief to hopelessness, to frustration and back to hopelessness again! I was pretty sure she had this condition, but I also knew that because it wasn't recognized in the diagnostic manuals, we would still be without a formal diagnosis. At this point, however, this was the least of my worries. I wondered if I would be able to cope with Jasmine's refusals forever. Despair began to settle in. I felt so low and exhausted.

A few weeks later, we arrived at the Wednesday night prayer meeting in church where I was met by the pastor. We exchanged the usual greetings, and I briefly mentioned how I thought life could be better right now! He asked me if I would like to be prayed for, and I accepted gratefully.

Andy and I were exhausted, and we stood together as our church family surrounded us, and they started to pray. I began to cry. Their prayers were so accurate. One lady described a picture of a lump of clay being pummelled and battered. This was a good analogy about how I was feeling! She went on to say that the clay was being moulded into a beautiful pot, full of purpose. Maybe, just maybe, this was all going to work out. Another person spoke out the words of Isaiah 40:31: '. . . those who hope in the LORD will renew their strength. They will soar on wings like eagles; they will run and not grow weary, they will walk and not be faint.' I needed to know that I could survive this parenting thing and I found the encouragement energizing. Another couple prayed for hope to return, and amazingly, it did! I woke the following day feeling much stronger. I was hopeful that life would bring enjoyment and fulfilment. This occasion had brought something very powerful and significant to me. Those prayers and prophecies were accurate and encouraging. Their impact had been so positive, and I wanted to be able to remind myself of them when I wobbled again!

If Jasmine did have PDA, I could see that I needed to move away from the idea of it being hopeless. Only hope would energize me to look for ways of dealing with the behaviours.

I reflected on the appointments I had with the behaviour nurse and the strategies she had encouraged me to use. She had been trying to show me another way of parenting, one I had failed to see up until now. I had been so busy fighting Jasmine's odd ways. I had been unaccepting and desperate to change them. I had been stuck in negativity and had wanted to control her to make her 'good'. Now I had a new revelation about how she saw the world. Anxiety was leading her, not disobedience.

I knew that the only way forward was through the supernatural power of God. I needed him to give me revelation, hope, self-control and patience in abundance. I realized that my patience needed to be limitless. This revelation enabled me to be creative with how I presented requests to Jasmine. Rather than saying, 'You need to brush your hair,' I would ask, 'Who would you like to brush your hair?' Other strategies seemed to work too. Such as, 'Shall we sing while I do this?' and 'Can you think of a word beginning with "B"?' The distractions and techniques were endless. They didn't always work so I would often find myself racking my brains to find another ploy to get her to do even the simplest of tasks. In the end, I would always have an idea that worked and I was seeing more success in our interactions.

When dealing with Jasmine, life was seen as a game. We were advised to have no hard and fast rules, but to bring a sense of fun whenever we could. We needed to be light-hearted and relaxed if we were going to parent her well. It didn't mean that this approach worked all the time, but it certainly gave us a fighting chance. Trying to love her unconditionally was something I wanted to aim for, but it wasn't always easy.

19

Stretched

It was late in 2014 and the evening was drawing in as the school bus drew up and tooted its horn outside our house. As Jasmine stepped out onto the pavement, I greeted her with a warm smile, 'Hello, darling.' Her eyes glared angrily at me and her feet pounded on the ground. She growled, 'Go away' as she stormed past me into the house. My senses alerted me that a potential meltdown was on its way. Jasmine had been to an afterschool club and it was now dinner time.

As we stood in the kitchen, her petite frame seemed double its size, emanating an aura which held the room and everything in it to ransom. Zoe and Georgia looked at me uneasily, as they were also being held captive to whatever Jasmine decided would happen next. Dinner was ready, and in solemn silence I distributed the ingredients onto the plates. Zoe made the drinks and Georgia rustled in the cutlery drawer for utensils. We all felt anxious. I dared to ask Jasmine if she felt unwell, but she was unable to say what was bothering her. However, she did accept some of the paracetamol that I offered her. As I put dinner on Jasmine's plate, she snarled, 'I don't want that.' I removed it, but she then said she did want it, so I put it back on the plate again. She did the same with the ketchup, which she usually liked. This was not so easy to remove from her plate; however, I gave it a go and it seemed to temporarily satisfy her agitation.

It was just the girls eating, as Andy was away on business. At the table, Jasmine started to dictate who would sit next to who, but we remained calm and took our usual seats, ignoring the aggressive demands placed upon us. Jasmine, unable to cope with us not doing as she told us, decided she would not have dinner and threw herself onto the sofa. In the light of our past experiences, we thought it was wise for us to give her some time to sit quietly and think.

We began to eat, feeling uncomfortable and aware that even after she had sat for a while, if we were to ask Jasmine to do anything it would be a challenge, even if it was in her best interests. We momentarily put Jasmine's agenda aside and tried to resume normal conversation about how our days had been. When she realized she was being ignored, Jasmine began to make a moaning noise, so in a soft voice I invited her to join us. After a few moments of her processing the request, she accepted the offer and sat up at the table sensibly. With great speed, she shovelled her food in, until there was only a small piece of chicken left. She had said nothing during this time, but now piped up in a demanding voice, 'I want ketchup.' I was still eating my meal so I suggested she finished her chicken with her drink if it was a bit dry, rather than my having to get up while I was eating.

Jasmine was outraged and threw her fork, which hit me on my forehead. I had reached my limit of patience at this point and everything within me was screaming out, 'Enough, this is just enough!' I hated how Jasmine should be controlling us all like this, even to the point of hurting one of us. Upset, cross and predicting the next possibilities of behaviour, I got up from my seat and went over to her to restrain her from further outburst or damage. She was too big, strong and angry for me, so this ended up exacerbating the situation rather than making it better. Jasmine, fuelled by what I thought was anger now, started reaching out for the dinner plates to throw them. Between us, we managed to clear the table of everything except one placemat which Jasmine took the opportunity to throw; it formed a hole as it hit the wall.

I shouted at her, 'Enough! I've had enough, stop this right now!' I felt my face flush as I goaded her with punching fists in the air. The adrenalin had kicked in by this point and, with what little self-control I had left, I walked away. Zoe and Georgia also retreated from the scene, frightened about what might happen next. We left the room and stood just the other side of the door, holding it closed. Jasmine followed, tried the door and, unable to open it, she continued her unplanned line of attack.

Hearing noise, I opened the door enough to see through a small opening. The kitchen sides were being cleared of the knives from dinner prep, a chopping board and everything else that happened to be there. Then she started to throw items from a box in the corner of the room. My instinct was to stop her from continuing this rampage. I stood staring through the crack in the door. I couldn't see how this was going to end, and took the decision to get a blanket and swaddle Jasmine to see if I could get her to calm down. Her anger was very powerful and it took all three of us some time to pin Jasmine down and swaddle her. In the process, her legs swung about, her hands lashed out to grab our skin, her face lurched towards us to try to take a bite. It was like we were dealing with a tormented animal.

The three of us were stressed, scared and unsure of what to do. Out of resources, I became mindful that we could pray for

God to intervene and diffuse the situation. As we prayed over her, Jasmine seemed to calm down, and I became very aware of how foreboding it must have been for her to have all three of us leaning over her. This didn't feel right, so I suggested the girls left the room and let Jasmine have some calm, undivided one-to-one attention. I offered Jasmine a hug, which she accepted, but within ten seconds, she had switched back into attack mode and was jabbing at my sides, trying to pinch me. I drew back and resisted, but she continued to hurt me. I needed help, nothing seemed to be working to bring this to an end, so I picked up the phone and dialled 999 for a police officer to come to our aid.

Once I was on the phone, I left the room, shut the door and resigned myself to the chance of further trashing and potential risk to Jasmine, but I put my safety as a priority. The emergency service person on the phone asked me a barrage of questions as to what had happened and, as I told her, I began to cry. I hadn't said much to the person before Jasmine opened the door and was standing in front of me, staring at me like a predator eyeing up its prey. I stopped speaking, but the voice on the phone was urging me to explain why I had called. I tried to tell them I couldn't speak, that it would start again if I described any more, but they insisted, so I did and it all started again. The kicking legs and punching fists came at me. I was by the front door, so I let myself out and shut it behind me.

I was upset, but safe, and still connected on the cordless phone. I could hear Jasmine crying and making crashing and banging noises in the hallway. There was a momentary silence before she began to kick the front door. This lasted a minute or so, and then it went quiet. Still on the phone and waiting for a police officer to arrive, I took a deep breath. A few quieter moments passed before I heard Jasmine call out, 'I'm sorry.'

My instinct told me that it was over. I hung up the phone, located the spare key and let myself back into the house. It looked like a tornado had devastated my home as I walked through the hallway and kitchen, which led me through to the back lounge. Here I found my little girl again, sitting on the sofa.

'Hi, Mum,' she said, as if nothing had happened.

The police officer arrived about five minutes later. By now it was a much calmer household. She took a few details and spoke to Jasmine about her behaviour. Jasmine agreed with her quite happily, seemingly oblivious to the chaos. The case was open and closed in a few short moments. It appeared to the policewoman that this had been a simple situation which had reached its own conclusion, and no further assistance was needed. The police officer left and I had to force myself to switch back to the friendly, loving parent so I could get Jasmine to comply with my instruction to go to bed. On the surface, I pretended. On the inside, I was broken again and feeling the trauma of abuse. I had to shelve my emotions for now, not only for Jasmine, but for Zoe and Georgia too. We were all traumatized.

As Jasmine got ready for bed, she resisted cleaning her teeth and putting on her pyjamas, although fortunately she did complete the tasks when I reminded her of what had just happened. Once she was in bed, I went in search of Georgia, who was in her bed crying softly. My heart broke for her; emotions were high for us both. I hugged her, wanting to console her and make it all OK. I felt torn between anger towards Jasmine and my protective feelings for Georgia. I listened to her tell me how she felt towards Jasmine, and I understood how hard it was for her. Jasmine took so much precedence in our home; she controlled so much of how life was, which made Georgia feel marginalized and set aside. This episode had just added fear into the mix too. I could see the importance of being real with our feelings while we talked, and the fear was very real, but I also felt that we needed to find something that could draw us to a better place. I posed the possibility that this experience would grow something within Georgia that would be of use for the future. She would be learning about compassion in the face of adversity, strength in a place of weakness, acceptance of others, even when they didn't seem to deserve it. I told her I thought she was amazing, I thanked her for supporting me and said that I believed she would be someone that people would be able to turn to when they themselves were in crisis because she would be able to relate to them. We both felt calmer after the conversation, and she decided she would like to go to see a friend down the road, so I let her go.

My next move was to check on Zoe. Being the eldest and having had to fight many of her own battles in the past, she was emotionally strong and very well-equipped with solutions to difficulties. But this situation had also hit her hard. I spent some time with her too, listening to her reflections on what had happened, and what we could have done to avoid it, and how we could make it better next time. I realized that earlier, I had been too hasty to react, and when I had decided on an action, that I needed to stick with it for longer rather than think that it wasn't working and move onto another strategy. I had confused Jasmine and I hadn't given her the time to settle into the technique we were using, and I also learnt that I needed to keep a distance from her. If I had left her with the initial trashing, rather than try to stop her, maybe it would have ended there, or if once we had swaddled her and she began to calm down, we had stayed with gentle voices calming her for longer, maybe that would have ended it. On reflection, it was the time she was left alone with no one to argue with or fight that she burnt herself out and calmed herself down. I learnt some valuable lessons in this. I was sorry to have got it wrong, but I felt more equipped for next time. I was grateful I had been able to have this conversation with Zoe, she was definitely gifted with wisdom and maturity beyond her 18 years.

The next day, I rang our social worker to tell her about what had happened. I wanted her to find out from me rather than from a police report. She suggested I rang the CAMHS team for them to decide whether it would be worth prescribing an emergency medication which might prevent a meltdown reaching this crescendo again. She also highlighted the potential danger that Jasmine could be in if she hurt herself somehow during a meltdown, which prompted a discussion about proper restraint procedures. After our call, I rang CAMHS and they gave us a sedative to use in emergencies.

A month later, we had to face another episode. I missed the warning signs this time, so it was too late to administer the calming medication as she was already out of control by the time I realized what was going on. I was ready with my plan of action this time. I went into an adjoining room to observe what was going on, while she swept round the kitchen and threw items on the floor. I had already decided to let her trash it and I would only intervene if she hurt herself. Zoe and Georgia had already retreated to their rooms, but Andy, on hearing the noise, came to see what was going on. I wondered if he felt he needed to rescue Jasmine from herself, as he tried to stop her. He tried to get her to tell him what was wrong, but she was unable to. She began to attack him. Her nails scratched down his arms and drew blood.

I couldn't bear to see this, so I called out from my safe place, 'Leave her!' but he persisted in trying to settle her. On seeing him make no progress with this, I called out again, 'Just leave her!' Fuelled with frustration and helplessness, he started towards me, trying to explain himself. Scared by the level of emotion, I fixed my eyes on the floor.

'We can't help her,' I said, quietly, 'she needs to do this herself. We need to stay out of her way until she ends this on her own.'

Andy begrudgingly accepted this and stormed upstairs. Jasmine followed him shortly afterwards, but went into her own room, shouting and crying.

After some time had passed, I went into her room and offered the medication again. She was beginning to calm down enough to be able to engage with what I was saying. She accepted the tablet and I told her she could come down when she was ready and calm. When she hadn't appeared after five minutes, I went up to check on her and she said she was ready to come down and clear up the mess that she had made. The sedative tablet seemed to have no obvious effect of drowsiness and she had finished her outburst by the time it had any chance to take effect, so I knew that next time I would need to give her a higher dose if I could anticipate a meltdown occurring in time!

After reflecting on these incidents, I found myself not being able to sleep one night as my mind was racing and I decided to write about how I was feeling. I entitled it, 'The Forest'.

It was like being in a dense forest. The trees huge and height foreboding. Their trunks so wide, it would take a few people to encircle them. The surface of each was rough and uneven, the pattern unique on every one.

Above me, numerous branches intertwined, impossible to decipher which arm belonged to which body. The darkness deep and the edges of the forest far from view. Light was trapped in upper places, unable to penetrate to the floor below.

I hid. I was in that dark place where the light could not reach. I stayed close to the large, old oak's trunk. The ground under my feet was soft and uneven. It was blanketed with rotten leaves, moss, broken twigs and probably crawling with life I had no desire to connect with.

The giant of the forest was searching for me and it seemed to know how to navigate the trees. It appeared oblivious of the dense thicket and took no notice of the absent path. It tramped with clumsy strides, confidently, towards me. From its mouth came a loud, roaring incomprehensible noise as it ducked below the branches and swung around the trunks.

I could feel the vibrations in my body from its movement as it got nearer. My skin prickled and my heart pounded, as terror and anticipation took authority over me and I knew I had been taken captive.

The giant paused. I held my breath. Silence hung in the air as it realized that it was at the end of its search. It was now beside me, peering down through the cage of branches that were my only protection. It could not reach me or devour me. Its hot breath curled all around me; I couldn't avoid it. It was not pleasant but it did not harm me. A drop of water fell through a branch and it dawned on me that the giant may have been crying.

I was trapped, my fear towered as high as the tree, the giant and beyond. My stomach twisted into a tight knot and my legs dared to hold me upright. My fear and frustration overwhelmed me and I stood frozen.

I could feel the damp roughness of the tree's jacket as I pressed myself against it. It supported me. I had nowhere to run, but I was grateful for the uncomfortable, harsh tree that was, at this time, the safest place to be. I felt fragile and I wished I could be anywhere else other than here.

I released my breath and drew a new one, telling myself to calm down and pull myself together. I needed to face the giant, face to face, and yet I just wanted to run. Run out of here and not look back.

Deep down, I knew that the giant would continue to follow me wherever I ran.

Trapped, I could see detachment was not an option, I needed to stay, be strong and accept my vulnerability.

My gloomy thoughts drew me to the light source above, which was confined by the mesh of pine needles and oak leaves. If only the light could break through, if only I could access it, it may help me see a way through this safely.

With a steadier heartbeat, a new perspective began to dawn. I realized that I had choice, I started to see there had always been choice. I might not have liked the choices, but I had never been denied the option to choose.

I could stay crippled with fear of the giant, or find some way to overcome it.

Until this point, I had been so wrapped up in my own world, I hadn't stopped to appreciate what it might look like from the giant's perspective. I had not even considered that the giant may be as fearful as me. I hadn't acknowledged that the giant was alone and may have been searching for companionship. I assumed it wanted to devour me, to take me over and victim-ize me but maybe, just maybe I was wrong . . . Maybe fear was the problem, not the giant?

As I stood there, aware of this position between us, I looked down to my feet. I could not look at the giant.

I was suddenly distracted as my eyes were stolen by a sudden movement just to the side of me. An awareness reawakened from within me to the life below that previously I had no desire to connect with. A tiny, shrew-like creature scampered through the leaf piles away from me, its eyes fixed open and sure about its goal. Clearly it knew its vulnerability, but was willing to take the risk of moving into an open space. Remaining stationary, my eyes followed its path, and somewhere along its trail, they collided with a shard of the light source from above. The creature paused for a moment as if it was collecting input, then it scurried away, behind a fallen branch, out of sight.

I began to raise my head, captured by the light shard. There was more than one. I had thought the place was dark, assuming the light was trapped somewhere above me. I hadn't noticed the light shards all around. They were like pins holding a design in place, each one strategically piercing across the forest floor.

Fascinated, energized and ready now, I lifted my eyes to look at the giant. I scanned the tree trunk and then the network of branches above, expecting to see a large pair of bulbous eyes, but instead I just saw more light. This place was brighter than I had realized. Squinting, I lifted my hand to shield its intensity.

Perplexed, I wondered where the giant had gone, but also aware that the knotted, twisted feeling in my stomach was unravelling. Something very strange was happening to me. My knees were vigorously shaking, and peace flowed over me. The fear that had gripped so tight, just ran away. An inner strength filled its place. I welcomed in peace and a warm sensation filled my body.

This moment could stay! The fight was over, I could rest and savour the moment.

My senses stirred to a familiar sound. The voice of my child speaking my name. She stepped out from behind the tree and asked to play. Resourcefully and purposely, I stepped forward and walked towards her. The giant had gone.

As the year progressed, we witnessed a number of positive changes. Jasmine's school was a very safe place for her to be.

Her teacher was excellent at understanding her and anticipated the things that she knew caused Jasmine to stumble. They had good staffing levels and the teacher used visual support aids to help Jasmine respond to demands; it was noted they needed to give Jasmine time to process the requests before they could get her to comply. The work at school was regularly focused on emotions and what to do about them when we face them. The concepts were fairly complex, but this teacher had a marvellous way about her that Jasmine was able to respond to – most of the time, anyway!

Parenting Jasmine continued to be hard work, and we felt very grateful for the support social services had offered us over the years. We had regular breaks; Jasmine had two 'tea visits' a week, and one evening each week, a carer would come in and wash her hair and get her into bed. Now, once a month we had a wonderful family who took care of her from Friday evening to Sunday afternoon. Life was manageable and a lot more enjoyable.

We continued under the care of CAMHS for medication, and a behaviour nurse specialist for advice on helping Jasmine extend her work on emotions. At one appointment, Jasmine was asked to tell the specialist what she knew about emotions and on her own, she was able to identify five different emotions, what happened when she felt them and what she could do about it when she experienced them. I was very impressed and felt hope rise again that we could overcome these difficulties in time.

I was learning how to respond more appropriately to Jasmine. Instead of seeing her behaviour as odd or wrong, I would make light of it with a joke and this seemed to have a positive result for our relationship. I think I began to accept her for who she was, instead of trying to fight it out of her. This meant I had more energy and there was more peace in our home.

I decided that I would pray for a month in Jasmine's room while she slept to see if this would help her further. One morning, towards the end of the month, she woke in a difficult mood. She spent a long time refusing to get up, she was rude and argumentative over breakfast, and she refused to put her shoes on or wear a jumper or coat in the cold weather. I was frazzled in my attempts to help her get ready for school. Finally, she was ready. The bus arrived, but she stopped and sat on the front doorstep and refused to move. I was at my wits' end as I drew close to her, asking her nicely to get on the bus. Then, she reached out to scratch me, so I backed off and managed to miss the bite that was also being offered. Her legs began to kick out and I asked her to be gentle, with no effect. I felt I should respond with the words, 'It's OK, Jasmine.'

In reality, her behaviour was far from OK. It wasn't OK with me that she should attack me like that and I'm sure it wasn't OK with her either. She would have felt remorseful about it later. However, these words had an amazing effect on Jasmine. I watched her as she physically relaxed, and I knew it was safe to embrace her. It was like the key had been found, and the door was unlocked. I held her briefly and she smiled and said, 'Bye, Mum, see you later.' I was left on the doorstep astounded by how we could go from one place to another so rapidly. I was happy that we had found a way forward this time.

This event opened my eyes to see the vast love that God had for Jasmine, even when she messed up and found herself in a state. Saying to Jasmine, 'Snap out of it. Sort yourself out. I don't like it when you do that,' would have had no benefit. Everything within me had once believed that this response would somehow make change happen, but in this moment the essence of love was what broke through and brought about positive change. My expression of love towards her enabled her to respond positively.

I was surprised at my response too, as it seemed the very opposite to what I should have said. I learnt that God had my back, he was always a faithful friend and a comforter to me. In Galatians chapter 6, I read about the Holy Spirit and how I was enabled to behave in an opposite mode to what was natural to me, and I learnt that if I lived to please God and that if I continued to carry on doing good works, then I would 'reap a harvest' of blessing. It was a reminder to me that I shouldn't give up on Jasmine because I could see good coming from all that I was learning and changing about myself. There had always been a way forward even when it hadn't seemed like it.

20

Questions with No Answers

In July 2016, Jasmine's refusals had increased in pattern. We were seeing less aggression, but the lock-in positions were part of our everyday lives. This was where Jasmine would sit with her head down and send the silent (but clear) message of, 'I can't do what you have suggested and I can't make choices from your options. I am stuck and I can't say or do anything right now.' These moments left me struggling to know what to do.

Going to the toilet, taking a drink, getting dressed and going to school are all normal events for a 14-year-old. Somehow Jasmine didn't have a natural desire to do these things, and she didn't cope with being asked to do them either, so what was I to do?

On this seemingly unending journey, social services were extremely supportive (as I mentioned earlier) as was the special needs behaviour nurse. I had so many questions: What was the diagnosis? What made Jasmine tick? We all have our own ways, so was it just her ways?

There was also the question of self-neglect. How much should you let someone make their own choice to neglect themselves and how much should you intervene and help them, especially when they have special needs? Jasmine was very capable – she just didn't think she was. That meant she continually sought assurance, and either asked someone to do things for her or she would refuse to do them altogether.

I was destined to be a parent. It was all I dreamt of as I grew up, and I know that I am blessed with my children. It seemed that my maternal heart was being prepared for this immense task, which I hope I have taken very seriously.

There have been times when I haven't known whether I was coming or going – we have seen such extremes of behaviours. I have been assured by the teams of professionals and friends that I'm not guilty of being a bad parent, and I am relieved about that.

In May 2016, I was putting Jasmine to bed and we were reading her children's Bible. The story we read was about the events between Moses and Pharaoh. Pharaoh had enslaved the Israelites, who were God's chosen people. Moses had been appointed by God to take the Israelites out of slavery and into a promised land. He repeatedly approached Pharaoh, asking him to let the people go, and each time he asked, he was met with a firm 'no'.

As I read this with Jasmine, I felt a familiar parallel to my own life. The words on these pages seemed to contain a power that surprised me. I had been crying out to God to let me out of this endless battle of 'No, no, no'. A month previously I had been encouraged by someone that I would be entering 'a promised land' soon. As I read this story, I felt heard by God, and so I took some time to reflect on what happened further in the story. God was on a mission to free his people from slavery and he wasn't discouraged by Pharaoh's negative response. The story continues with Pharaoh and his people experiencing rivers of blood, plagues of frogs, locusts and finally the deaths of all Egyptian first-born sons. This resulted in Pharaoh's eventual consent to release the Israelites.

As I reflected on this story, I thought blood, locusts, frogs and the deaths of children were extreme measures for God to allow in order to bring freedom to his people. I realized that in my own life I had felt like a slave. I wondered if God could release me from the challenges I was facing. A thought came to my head that maybe it would turn out OK, even if extreme measures were needed to get there.

Two months passed and morning after morning we were greeted with the familiar and aggressive refusal to get up and get ready for school. During this time, we had been given carers to help us two mornings a week, but even with the extra help, if Jasmine did get up, she would refuse to get ready or she would get ready and then refuse to get on the bus. I was beginning to think that I could not carry on in this way. I started to think to myself, 'If she keeps this up, she will have to go and live somewhere else. I'm not doing this any more.' One morning, I was feeling so frustrated with her, these thoughts became actions.

On this particular morning, Jasmine had eventually got out of bed and come downstairs. She had eaten her breakfast and was sitting at the breakfast bar with her drink and tablets in front of her. She was wearing her pyjamas and seemed to have no intention of getting dressed or going to the toilet. The bus for school arrived and beeped its horn. I told her I was happy to help her get ready, but I couldn't help her if she didn't let me. I had tried the fun, the bribes, gentle persuasion to try to coax her into getting ready, but she was just not going to comply. The thoughts I had been having gained momentum and I left her at the breakfast bar, went upstairs and packed a bag with everything she might need for a few days away. I confronted her with the choice of going to school or going to live somewhere else.

Jasmine said she wanted to live somewhere else.

I waved the school bus away and told Jasmine to go and get in the car. She willingly did so and beckoned me to join her. Before I left, I popped my head into Andy's home office and told him I was taking her to social services. He was shocked and went to the car to speak to Jasmine. She did not want to engage with him, so he returned and told me he wasn't happy about this. I felt awful. I drove Jasmine to social services and handed her over. I still can't quite believe that I did it. I drove her in my car, everything within me saying, 'What are you doing? You can't do this!' But something within me was compelling me to keep going.

I had been saying to Jasmine for a few weeks, 'If you keep refusing, then I can't care for you and you'll have to go and live somewhere else.' These were not words that came easily, but when I'd exhausted the creative bank of fun, bribes, incentives, negative consequences, gentle persuasion, prayer, distraction techniques, crazy ideas, ringing others to get them to speak with her, and leaving her to her own devices, what options was I left with?

In a way, this had been inevitable and I knew I had to carry it out, even though I didn't know what the consequences would be. However, I was reminded of the thought that it would be OK to be extreme. We arrived at social services with a holdall and Jasmine in her pyjamas. I asked for the duty social worker and miraculously, our own social worker arrived. Within an hour, there was a bed available just down the road that had staff available to care for Jasmine. So off she went. All of this was her choice. I didn't force her to do anything, because I couldn't do that!

'Bye, Mum, see ya!' She was on her way, just like that.

I felt strange; emotionally torn. A part of me was satisfied that this was a right outcome and that there was hope that life would become easier. The other part of me was saying, 'What kind of mother does that to their child?' I felt relieved and bereft all at the same time. When I got home, I told Andy how sorry I was to go against his wishes. I told him the outcome of the visit to social services and he was relieved that they'd said Jasmine would be returning home.

Jasmine stayed there for twenty-four hours, which took us to our pre-booked appointment with a psychiatrist at CAMHS. The behaviour nurse was also there, along with our social worker, Andy and myself. We had never met this psychiatrist before and this wasn't a great place to make any changes needed to improve life for us all. I'm not sure I connected very well with her either, which was a little disappointing.

I believed we needed a serious conversation about medication and making changes, but the subject was given very little time for discussion as the psychiatrist needed to get to know Jasmine first, rather than start with medication changes. I could see her perspective, but this was very difficult for us when we had been saying for a while that things weren't working. However, when pushed, it was decided that we would trial Jasmine on half her medication to see if it was having any effect on her.

The other thing that frustrated me about the meeting was that when PDA was mentioned, it was dismissed straightaway as a condition that doesn't have medical recognition. That aside, whether it was recognized or not, there were a number of key issues being presented that gave a lot of insight into the world as Jasmine saw it, which were very relevant in seeing a way forward.

After the appointment, we took back responsibility of Jasmine and delivered her to school. She returned home later that day on her school bus, with a clear desire to please. As I observed her, one of the things that I found interesting was the insight she had into herself. She knew she had got 'stuck' because she told me. She also asked me what she should do if she got stuck again, and was able to recall one of the strategies we had used in the past. I saw this as very promising for Jasmine managing herself in the future.

At a meeting with school the following week, we discussed how it was working for her there. It was agreed that they were meeting her needs, and she was doing very well with all the techniques and adaptations they had made to make it work best for her. The effects of this would unfold in time.

So, we would remain with the support of social care and provision at this school – through good times and bad.

21

I Think I'm Learning

'You're gorgeous.' Her arms reached around my waist, and she squeezed me tight. Her chin rested on my chest, her face tilting upwards as she looked up at me. 'I love you, Mum,' she uttered for the fourth time.

'I love you too, Jas. You're wonderful,' I said.

She grinned and in a silly voice said, 'No, I'm not, you are.'

The banter between us led to her calling me Obed and me calling her Thumbelina and we both laughed at the ridiculousness of it. Our relationship had really grown, and we had found new levels of relating to each other. Humour was our number one hit.

I was grateful to experience better times with Jasmine. Finally, the good times began to outweigh the bad. I had observed so much about the way in which Jasmine processed life, and with the help of our support network, I had found ways of finding space from the responsibility of caring for her. Our respite package was good. We now had a night a week during term-time at a local centre. We had carers three times a week coming to the house. We had our two tea visits a week at Julie's with Amy and Christina and we had a Friday and Saturday evening once a month with her foster carers. We also accessed a Saturday club once a month. In the school holidays we had a day a week with a carer. Not caring for her 24/7 meant that we could go for longer periods of times where we were just able to enjoy being together. I was able to appreciate the good things about her, like her helpfulness towards others and her sense of humour. Her noes were still present but considerably less; maybe this was due to how we worded requests and maybe it was also due to her learning how to navigate life's demands. One thing I noted was that with the work we had been doing with the fruits of the Spirit and teaching her about emotions, her emotional intelligence had matured beyond her intellectual intelligence. This now stood her in good stead to be able to identify her emotion and be able to respond to it in a more appropriate manner, rather than just having a meltdown about it.

The box looked like a tumbling waterfall with paper overhanging the edge and pens scattered messily around its perimeter. It was Sunday afternoon and Jasmine had decided to make some cards for her friends. She unpacked the box further, looking for the right kind of card to use. She delved deeper while she searched for stickers for decoration. Having found what she wanted, she gathered it all together in her arms and launched it on to the table to begin her task. She sat sideways on her chair, and I could see the delight on her face to be using her new thin, fibre-tipped pens for the writing inside. I sat with her, watching her write, and resisted her demand to help when she could do it herself. She loved doing this; it was one of her favourite activities. I admired her as she pushed through her difficulties, and I repeatedly encouraged her that she could do it. One of her challenges was that poor muscle control in her hands made them tire easily, but her determination to send some cards saying, 'You're wonderful, love Jasmine', drew her to completion. She was so pleased with her work that she didn't want to be separated from them. The cards went to bed with her and she slept with them under her pillow! Dog-eared, the next day they journeyed to the breakfast table and onto the school bus and finally reached their destination: into the hands of her friends.

One of the threads that I can see throughout our story is that Jasmine has brought people together. It has taken more than one person to care for her holistically. Teamwork has been able to offer Jasmine different styles of care, which I believe has made her world richer. This has highlighted the importance of community, and I'm blessed to be able to have been a giver and receiver over the years. It could have been so easy to isolate myself when life was tough, as I could have perceived myself to be a burden on others. On our own, we have little protection against self-pity and doubt; we can become slaves to anxiety and depression. At times I have nearly given up; but with other people, who wanted to help and to share in my pain, togetherness enabled me to survive.

I have come to see that Jasmine has been a gift to be shared. I'm told by the people who care for her that they love being with her as she has a great sense of humour, she's kind, helpful and she enjoys the simplicities of life. In her book *The Hiding Place*, Corrie ten Boom says that 'God values us, not our strength or our brains but simply because He has made us' (NY: Bantam Books, 1974). Jasmine was made with a purpose, and while it has been and continues to be a challenge, many good things have happened through her.

Life is a journey, so we are always in process, and I'm experiencing more agreement from Jasmine and shorter timeframes from being stuck to being able to motivate herself. I'm still hoping to see more of the miraculous hand of God transforming Jasmine's 'no' to 'yes', and for her to feel free in her world, where she can overcome the anxiety and, at times, panic, that stop her from enjoying the things she really loves.

Motherhood has taught me what love means. I've been challenged to love unconditionally, which was easy with Zoe and Georgia, but more difficult with Jasmine, as there were times when I just wanted her to go away. But she has been one of my greatest teachers. Managing her behaviour, over many years, has been massively challenging, and I've often questioned what it has all been about. I can see now that she has given me opportunity to think about the wider issues of life, as well as learning to know and love myself and others.

Being Mum to my three girls has been an honour and a privilege. Guiding Zoe, Georgia and Jasmine through childhood showed me I could never control anyone, but that I had influence on the choices they made. It was important for me to consider wisely how I interacted with them. Time passed so quickly, and as I embraced Zoe and Georgia's teenage years, I made it my goal to keep our relationship as good as we could. I would seek them out when they spent long periods of time in their bedrooms, to show them I valued being with them. I would listen to their questions about life and occasionally answer with questions, so they could discover things for themselves. Sometimes I would offer my opinion, but I wanted to give them the space and freedom to find their own answers too. I wanted them to know that their voice was valid and important, even if we didn't always agree. It has been a joy and a challenge to balance my desires for them beside their desires for themselves.

Diabetes has continued to be challenging, but Zoe has found a place for it in her life which means she's not governed by it. Her thyroid was blasted with radioactive iodine when she was 17 so that was stabilized by thyroxine replacement. At the age of 18, Zoe decided to go to South Africa on a mission trip to support a community needing guidance and support.

She raised her own money and booked her place with a group of people she had never met and spent three months serving others. She is currently living in Denmark studying at a college there. I'm content to know that I've brought up a child, and now a young woman, who carries some deep, valuable qualities within her, and I look forward with anticipation to seeing her future unfold.

Georgia, an introvert by nature, has grown into an amazing young lady. She is quietly confident, and I've seen her be someone who people turn to when they are struggling with a season in their life. The challenging days of her little sister limiting the quality connection with her mum and dad have stretched her and given her a compassion for those who also have had to contend with extra issues going on in their lives. I would have liked to have been a better mum to Georgia, but was relieved that, when I realized there were things I could do better, addressed them, and put them right, it wasn't too late. I remembered when my dad started saying, in my thirties, how wonderful he thought I was and how proud he was of me, that encouragement felt so good. I noted I didn't do this enough for Georgia when she refused to tell me she loved me because it was weird! It took a while, and a few conversations about it, for her to return my love, which could have been different if I had modelled it in her earlier years. We now have a flourishing relationship which has the qualities of a lovely friendship too.

Spiritually, I have grown so much in my faith. I've come full circle, from a small seed of faith, to questioning if it is all real, to now having faith to believe in miracles and that there really is a God who loves and cares for me and his world.

My marriage is still a work in progress. Our life together has been such a rocky road, full of pain and frustration. The journey we have experienced caused us to drift apart. We have been having counselling for the last two years and it is helping us get back on track and find each other again. Life has thrown us many curveballs and I think it's miraculous we've come this far! I have hope that we will come to a place where we are able to relate well to each other, and to love with everything we have.

My church's teaching has given me strategies to use which have helped me to keep going. I remember hearing a message about being a prisoner of hope – my faith in God would make me a prisoner of hope. I would always have something to keep hoping for, and this would keep me striving to see my dreams realized. This hope has protected me from cynicism and despair. Believe me, I have had times when hopelessness has knocked on my door and I have invited it in and allowed it to dwell there. While it stayed, it drained the life out of me and made me want to give up. I have learnt that when I focus on the fact that hope has captured me, I am able to get back up again with renewed strength and determination for better days ahead.

When we lost our son, Daniel, I thought I would never recover. My heart was so broken, I could never imagine a day without the constant nagging pain in my chest. Today, I can honestly say that I am healed. I don't feel that pain any more. Occasionally I'm overcome by what may have been, and I wonder what life would have been like if he had survived, but my pain has gone. I believe one of God's desires is for us to experience healing because I have experienced this. My loss made me appreciate life so much more and that I should hold all things lightly, as one day they could be there and the next day they could be gone. I've come to see that life owes me nothing, and I can be grateful for everything I have. In time, I have grown a strength that has enabled me to support others in their grief, which has helped me to see purpose in such tragedy.

I have also received healing for being told I was 'ugly' all those years ago. Someone once said to me, quoting a writer called Margaret Wolfe Hungerford, 'Beauty is in the eye of the beholder', and it made me see that I had been believing someone else's opinion of me. I realized that their opinion was subjective, and I was grateful to be able to rise above it and move on. I can also see healing in the relationship I had with my dad. Knowing what I know now, and spending time in reflection, helps me to see the bigger picture. Our two lives were connected at my birth. As a parent now myself, I know there were no rulebooks on how to be a dad, and even if there had been, life is no textbook. Dad did love me from the moment I arrived. We spent my childhood testing and learning all about relationships. We both failed and succeeded and, in the end, we have managed to create a relationship devoted to each other's wellbeing. It has taken years of pain and joy, but now we are richer in spirit and have a deep-rooted love and appreciation for each other.

The presence of anxiety has had a massive impact on my life, and I'm relieved that I have been able to find some ways of dealing with it. I recognize the importance of positive thinking, and that I need to be aware of my negative thoughts and challenge them with positive ones. A few years ago, I would get in the shower every day and wonder what part of my body had something wrong with it. I realized this wasn't giving me life and that these thoughts just fed my anxiety, so then I would tell myself, 'I'm healthy and I'm going to live a long life.' Initially, I would then argue with myself – how did I know that I was healthy and was going to live a long life? As time passed, however, the answer to my question became less important, and I found that I did start believing myself. Now, whether I'm believing a lie or not, I am free from the anxiety that used to plague me.

I have seen the faithfulness of God's promises in miraculous signs such as rainbows, angelic singing, God's whisper in the night, quotations from Scripture that have inspired me to press on and encouraged me that God is watching over me. I have also learnt that there is so much more to life and faith that I have yet to experience, which I will do with God who is ever-present, ever-loving and ever-redemptive, and I know that nothing is impossible for him to deal with.

The latter journey with Jasmine has trained me in supporting others, learning to love unconditionally and accepting that everybody's journey is unique. I've learnt how to be patient and kind in the face of adversity. I have experienced what it's like to be at the end of myself, thinking I couldn't possibly carry on caring for her, but significantly, she has taught me how to choose hope from a place of despair and how to love when everything within me wants to reject her. I am mindful when judging others and I believe in looking for the good in people. Jasmine has shown me that everyone has a purpose and a part to play in this tangled web we call life.

I marvel when I experience answers to my prayers. I have noticed that when Jasmine refuses and I take myself away to pray for her, I see an immediate response of her saying yes. This has not happened overnight, and it's taken years of me pleading for things to change, but I am seeing change now, which brings me joy on several levels. I've prayed for Jasmine, sometimes intently, sometimes not at all, and sometimes with the words, 'Help me, Lord.' I've prayed with more specifics, such as: 'Please create new neural pathways in her brain to enable her to make choices that bring her life and happiness.' I've begun to see change and now, as a teenager, she is more able to manage herself, name her emotion and be able to 'fix' herself. She tells me and others how gorgeous they are, and has me in fits of giggles when she engages in conversation. I'm filled with indescribable joy when she helps serve a meal to guests and chats to them like they're family members. I'm in no doubt that we are heading into happier times.

I have dreams, and I feel the next season is about realizing those dreams. I want to use everything I have learnt so far about life to help others to be equipped to live their lives in the best way they can. I desire that people know their value, purpose and gifting, and for them to enjoy life despite the storms that come their way.

I am grateful for my story. I'm a great believer that there are two sides to every coin. Where there is pain and sorrow, there is also joy and hope. Where there is negativity and loss, there is also positivity and gain. I believe we all have a choice to search for the flip side and I believe we all can possess a hope to find a way through. We can do life on our own but, inevitably, we come to points in our lives where we need someone or something to lean on.

This world offers us so much. There are groups and charities to support people in all sorts of areas of need. There are individuals we have unique relationships with, who build us up and encourage us. There are people with varying degrees of experience who are experts in their fields. Charities are often set up because of unfulfilled needs so, where there was pain, discomfort or loss, someone has decided not to be beaten by their situation and started to make a difference for others.

We have the freedom to choose what we lean on in the difficult times. I have become very aware of our freedom of choice and the effect that this has on our lives, both individually and as a society. We all make choices, whether they're good or bad; and, whether we're aware of them or not, they shape our existence and affect our destiny.

My experience is that in the dark times, where there just seemed to be no way forward and I've felt trapped, there has always been a solution or an answer or an opportunity to learn something new.

My journey of faith has grown with God's Spirit in partnership with my choice. I have been shown, and have chosen to believe in, a creator God, who is mighty in power, abounding in love and who has given me free will and has chosen to forgive me for my mistakes. I believe God has shown me a bigger picture, given me answers to my questions and has helped me to understand him more. I have been directed to a life full of purpose and value. This belief system has been the source of my ability to cope with everything that has come my way. I believe all that has happened has had a divine purpose that is for my benefit and not my downfall, and I'm grateful for it all.

I feel very blessed to have my life. I feel glad to have survived, and I am expectant with hope for what the future will hold. I will always continue to hope.

> . . . those who hope in the LORD
> will renew their strength.
> They will soar on wings like eagles;
> they will run and not grow weary,
> they will walk and not be faint.
>
> Isaiah 40:31

THOSE who hope in the LORD will renew their strength. They will soar — on wings — like eagles; they will run and not grow weary, they will walk and not be faint.

ISAIAH 40:31

Acknowledgements

Firstly, I want to thank Evelyn Gunn for helping me get this book from paper to computer and for encouraging me along the way.

Julie, Simon, Amy, Christina and Josh Hayes: Thank you for being our friends and for receiving us and in particular, Jasmine, into your family. Julie, thank you for doing life with me and helping me survive.

Mum and Dad: Thank you for loving me, encouraging me, challenging me and accepting me.

Ruth Clark: Thank you for our prayer times and support. You have helped shape my journey.

Jude Thomas: Thank you for sharpening me, I am richer for meeting you.

My family at Equippers Church: I have been encouraged, I have been taught, I have grown, I have discovered who I am meant to be. I will be eternally grateful.

My friends at Heathervale Baptist church: You journeyed beside me, you picked me up when I fell down and you helped me to build some solid foundations. Thank you.

My proof readers: Thank you Sheena Koop, Julie Hayes, Mum and Dad and Evelyn Gunn.

My editors, Mark Stibbe and Sheila Jacobs: Thank you for helping me to get my manuscript to read well.

Lucy Roberts: Thank you for the time you've taken to read the manuscript and sketch possibilities for the front cover.

My three social workers, you know who you are! I am so grateful to you. Thank you.

White Lodge Centre: Thank you for being a safe place, for supporting us and for accepting us for who we are.

NHS: You have provided well. The professionals we have met along the way have made it work for us. We are grateful.

Ruth and Phil Barker: Thank you, you are a treasure. Thank you for being a significant family to Jasmine. So grateful for all you have poured out.

Sally and Andrew Nash: Sally for your love and support, particularly for Georgia in the early days of Jasmine's life and Andrew, your prayers; they were instrumental in changing our direction to better parenting.

My loving Father God and your Son, Jesus, who have shown me that death is not the end. Thank you for the strength you've given me. Your Spirit has helped me by giving me inspiration, love, joy, peace, patience, kindness, goodness, gentleness, faithfulness and self-control. You are a good, good God. I couldn't have survived and conquered life without you.

EDITOR'S NOTE: Neither the author nor Authentic Media condone the use of 'hot saucing' as a method of controlling or modifying behaviour.

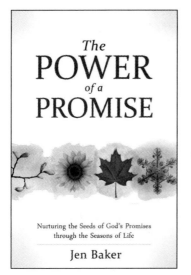

The Power of a Promise

Nurturing the seeds of God's promises through the seasons of life

Jen Baker

God loves to sow promises in our hearts, but they very rarely come to fruition immediately. Too often the storms of life can rob us of our hope, and we can give up on these promises. But what if these dark times were all part of the journey to fulfilled promises – would that give us hope to persevere?

Using a seed as a metaphor for the journey, Jen Baker shares six key stages a promise undergoes on its way to fulfilled purpose. Each stage of the journey is detailed, including what to expect and how we could respond.

Weaving together biblical reflections and real-life experiences, Jen inspires us to look at how we can all live fully in the calling God has uniquely designed for each of us.

978-1-78078-986-6

3

The Power of the Blessing

If you belong to Christ, then you are Abraham's seed, and heirs according to the promise.

Gal. 3:29

Behind the Scenes

By the time I was three years old I had mastered the pout.

My bottom lip was always on standby and within a moment's notice it could march forward, stand to attention, and defend self-pity till its dying breath. I was the younger sibling and it was always on high alert with my sister around, as competition only fuelled its fury. So, when our family fishing trip to Wisconsin found my sister and me standing on the dock fishing with our father, I was prepared.

I gave it time, fixing my eyes on the tiny, wobbling bobber underneath my watchful gaze, just waiting for my bite. This was my time; I could feel it.

'I got one!' I heard my sister yell. I ignored her and stared harder at my bobber, willing it to go under the water.

A few minutes later I heard her squeal 'I got one!'

Not long after, she cheerfully exclaimed 'Daddy, I got another one!'

Life was not going according to my three-year-old plan. Putting down my pole I walked over to peruse her haul of fish. I couldn't believe it – she was catching all my fish.

Pout time.

Looking up at my father I adamantly declared 'I can't do it' . . . lip wide enough for a seagull landing.

'Just try again,' my father suggested while busying himself around me.

Head down, pout out, I declared: 'No, it won't work – she's catching all my fish!'

Kneeling down to my level, my father gently said once again, 'Just try one more time. I bet this time you'll catch something . . .'

Looking into his smiling eyes I gently took his hand, walked to the pole he handed me and tried again. Time stood still as I looked down to see – my bobber had disappeared! I glanced up at my father, who smiled and said, 'Well, go on then – pull it up!'

At that moment my sister could have had a ship full of fish – I didn't care. I had finally caught . . . my fish.

(Fast forward thirteen years.)

Our family was sitting around at dinner time and we began talking about that family holiday and fishing together. I nonchalantly mentioned the fish I had finally caught after so many tries and how pleased I was with my catch. Suddenly I noticed the dinner table grow quiet, stolen glances moving between my sister/mom/dad. Finally I heard my dad gently say, 'I thought you knew.'

'Knew what?' I asked while chewing my dinner.

'*Ummm* . . . well . . . you see . . . I . . . well, your sister had so many fish that when your back was turned I just reached over and . . .'

(Insert time standing still.)

'All these years I've been catching . . . my sister's fish!' I shrieked.

The phrase 'bubble bursting' was made for moments like that.

But one day as I was preparing a message, the Lord brought that (still bruised) memory to mind, and gently showed me the Father's heart. I saw that it was my father's idea to go fishing, therefore my father would do whatever necessary to bring about the desire of his little girl's heart, because it was also his desire for her. And I realized my heavenly Father will work behind the scenes, doing whatever he needs to do, in order to bring about the desires he has planned for my life, using the abundance of others when necessary, knowing that in the future I would be the one sharing the harvest.

The Blessing

The blessing of the promised fish that day reminds me of Jesus telling Peter to pay his taxes by casting his hook and bringing in the first fish he catches, for the money he needed would be in the mouth of the fish (Matt. 17:24–27). I imagine Jesus grinning from ear to ear as he watched Peter give him a 'You're kidding, right?' look, just before hauling in the miraculous pro-vision. God's ways are truly beyond ours, and his possibilities are endless when it comes to provision and blessing. As we close out this chapter I want to remind us of our heritage in Christ, because it is within that heritage that the power of our promises begins taking root.

Deuteronomy 28 is a well-known chapter on the blessings of God. It outlines what we can expect if we walk in obedience to the Lord and his word, things such as blessing over our homes, finances, health and families. Of course, we live in a fallen world and, as we have seen, the enemy will always be there to steal, kill and destroy the intended blessing, but there is a blessing God longs to give us regardless. Proverbs 10:22 ESV says: 'The blessing of the LORD makes rich, and he adds no sorrow with it.'

> 'The blessing of the LORD makes rich, and he adds no sorrow with it' (Prov. 10:22 ESV).

The first words God spoke to Adam and Eve were a blessing as he told them to 'multiply' (see Gen. 1:28). After the flood we see the same words when God blessed Noah and said his family were to 'be fruitful and increase in number' (Gen. 9:1). And there are many more scriptures we could add here; in summary: God loves to bless!

One of the best-known passages on blessing is found a few chapters later in Genesis 12:1–3:

> The LORD had said to Abram, 'Go from your country, your people and your father's household to the land I will show you. I will make you into a great nation, and I will bless you; I will make your name great, and you will be a blessing. I will bless those who bless you, and whoever curses you I will curse; and all peoples on earth will be blessed through you.'

Galatians 3:16 says: 'The promises were spoken to Abraham and to his seed. Scripture does not say "and to seeds", meaning many people, but "and to your seed", meaning one person, who is Christ.' If Christ was Abraham's seed, and if we are in Christ, then we are heirs of all the blessings he received. We see this in Galatians 3:29 of the New Testament: 'If you belong to Christ, then you are Abraham's seed, and heirs according to the promise.'

I remember when this truth first started to resonate in my spirit and I grabbed hold of it, not by looking at my circumstances for confirmation, but rather looking at God's word for clarification, of how he intended me to live – the result was clearly blessed and as a blessing. Like any good father, God loves to bless his children, but he also expects his children to be like their heavenly Father, blessing the world around them. Abraham waited for twenty-five years to see his blessing begin to take shape, Jesus waited for thirty years to begin his ministry and we might need to wait even longer for our desired dreams to become reality. Yet both saw their promise fulfilled and blessing multiplied to the next generation – this is our heritage as believers in Christ.

So . . . How's Your Heart?

The first part of this book has intentionally focused on cultivating a rich, fortified soil because, as I have said several times for emphasis, without good soil you will not reap a strong harvest – naturally or spiritually. We all have seeds of promise given to us, both generally in the word and more specifically through our unique purpose, and as we begin exploring the process those seeds undergo to bring forth life, we must first be honest about the soil of our hearts.

As much as the Lord wants to bless us – and he does – he cannot bless disobedience. And it would be unfair to speak about a rich heritage without being honest about the consequences of a disobedient heart. Staying in line with our theme of the seed, we read in Galatians 6:7: 'Do not be deceived: God cannot be mocked. A man reaps what he sows.' We cannot sow to the flesh and expect to reap in the Spirit. It is simply impossible. So, let's take a moment for an honest inventory of our hearts.

I would be remiss if I didn't say upfront that above all, the key to rich soil is a strong, personal relationship with Jesus Christ. He is the one who makes life worth living. I grew up knowing about him, but I didn't realize I could know him personally, as a friend, for many years. I remember the day I finally chose to surrender my life, goals and dreams to him; it was the best decision of my life. I was a Resident Assistant at my university, which meant that I was in charge of a group of girls a year younger than me in their halls of residence.[1] Soon after they arrived I discovered most of them were Christians, and as I was studying for a degree in theatre, I created my own theatre assignment – to convince them I too was a Christian. I like to tell people I lied my way into Christianity.

> The key to rich soil is a strong, personal relationship with Jesus Christ.

As the weeks went by and I 'faked' my Christianity, I found myself becoming more and more interested. So, one day when walking with one of the girls, I casually asked how she would help someone become a Christian, taking mental notes as she talked. A few days later, alone in my bedroom, I gave God my name/birthdate/address/phone number (I assumed Jen Baker was a common name, so he might need some assistance finding the right one) . . . and waited sixty seconds for him to find me across the universal divide. After that it became a bit of a blur as I fumbled my way through a prayer, feeling like a fool and finally squeaking out an amen. I asked him to clarify that he had heard me by releasing a bit of lightning into the sky – lightning seemed like a 'God-tool' he would have on standby.

Nothing happened. I felt even more foolish. So, I got angry, swore like a sailor and went to bed thinking it was all a load of rubbish. Two weeks later I had a horrible day, decided to pick up a Bible . . . and haven't put it down since. The first time I read the Bible I realized *something* had changed, though I could not verbalize what. All I knew was that I experienced a peace inside I had not felt before and that I could have sat and read the word for hours. It was as if a veil had been removed and I could see clearly for the first time in my life. I have told the Lord numerous times that 'my life is not my own', and he knows I mean it.

It was on that basis that I sold everything, moved countries, overcame fears, stood on platforms, wrote books and followed the cloud multiple times to new locations and fresh assignments. What a journey it has been, full of promises – some fulfilled and some I am still holding near my heart thirty years later, wondering if they will ever come to pass.

Whether the promise has been received or is still in the waiting room, I continue to believe, because I have learned that it is daily decisions such as that which decide the direction of my future.

So, how much access to your heart does God have? Are there any rooms he is not allowed to enter? Richness of relationship is what ultimately grows richness of soil, producing the best environment for promises to be grown. He is a gentleman and will never push his way into our hearts, but at an invitation he will move in with grace, peace and love – one step at a time.

If you desire to become a Christian, or to re-dedicate your life to Christ, please see the prayer in the 'Author's Note' at the end of the book. I promise, inviting him in to your heart is the best decision you could ever make.

For reflection

- How do you feel knowing that God *desires* to bless you? How has he tangibly shown you those blessings over the years? (Take some time to give him praise and thanksgiving!)

- What seeds are you choosing to plant into good soil today? What kind of harvest are you believing to see?

- At the end of this chapter I asked: how much access to your heart does God have? How would you answer that question?

  If you have never prayed to receive Christ, or perhaps have walked away from the faith, I would encourage you to pray the salvation prayer found in the Author's Note. And then please send me an email and let me know so that I can rejoice with you!

Authentic

We trust you enjoyed reading this book from Authentic. If you want to be informed of any new titles from this author and other releases you can sign up to the Authentic newsletter by scanning below:

Online:
authenticmedia.co.uk

Follow us: